I0022750

Colley Cibber

The Ladies' Philosophy

A Comedy

Colley Cibber

The Ladies' Philosophy
A Comedy

ISBN/EAN: 9783744711319

Printed in Europe, USA, Canada, Australia, Japan

Cover: Foto ©Thomas Meinert / pixelio.de

More available books at **www.hansebooks.com**

BELL'S EDITION.

THE

E F U S A L;

OR, THE

LADIES PIHLOSOPHY.

A . C O M E D Y,

As written by COLLEY CIBBER.

DISTINGUISHING ALSO THE

ARIATIONS OF THE THEATRE,

AS PERFORMED AT THE

Theatre-Royal in Covent-Garden.

Regulated from the Prompt-Book,

By PERMISSION *of the* MANAGERS,

By Mr. WILD, Prompter.

PROLOGUE.

Spoken by the Author.

GAllants! behold before your eyes the wight,
Whose actions stand accountable to-night,
For all your dividends of profit or delight.
New plays resemble bubbles, we must own,
But their intrinsic value soon is known,
There's no imposing pleasure on a town.
And when they fail, count o'er his pains and trouble,
His doubts, his fears, the poet is a bubble.
As heroes by the tragic muse are sung;
So to the comic, knaves and fools belong:
Follies, to-night, of various kinds we paint,
One, in a female philosophic faint,
That wou'd by learning nature's laws repeal,
Warm all her sex's bosoms to rebel,
And only with Platonic raptures swell.
Long she resists the proper use of beauty,
But flesh and blood reduce the dame to duty.
A coxcomb too of modern stamp we show,
A wit——but impudent——a South-Sea beau.
Nay, more——our muses fire (but, pray, protect her)
Roasts, to your taste, a whole South-Sea director.
But let none think we bring him here in spite,
For all their actions, sure, will bear the light;
Besides, he's painted here in height of power,
Long ere we laid such ruin at his door:
When he was levee'd, like a statesman, by the town,
And thought his heap'd-up millions all his own.
No, no; stock's always at a thousand here,
He'll almost honest on the stage appear.
Such is our fare, to feed the mind our aim,
But poets stand, like warriors, in their fame;
One ill day's work brings all their past to shame.
Thus having tasted of your former favour,
The chance seems now for deeper stakes than ever.
As after runs of luck, we're most accurst,
To lose our winnings, than have lost at first;
A first stake lost has often sav'd from ruin,
But on one cast to lose the tout——is hard undoing.
But be it as it may——the dye is thrown,
Fear now were folly——Pass the Rubicon.

DRA-

DRAMATIS PERSONÆ.

MEN.

Covent-Garden.

Sir *Gilbert Wrangle*,	Mr. Macklin.
Frankly,	Mr. Lewis.
Granger,	Mr. Mahon.
Wittling,	Mr. Lee Lewes.
Cook,	Mr. Dunſtall.

WOMEN.

Lady *Wrangle*,	Mrs. Green.
Sophronia,	Mrs. Leſſingham.
Maid,	Miſs Ambroſe.
Charlotte,	Miſs Macklin.

Servants, &c.

THE

REFUSAL.

⁎ *The lines diſtinguiſhed by inverted comas, ' thus,' are omitted in the Repreſentation, and thoſe printed in Italics are the additions of the Theatre.*

ACT I.

The SCENE, *Weſtminſter-Hall.*

Frankly *and* Granger *meeting.*

FRANKLY.

IS it poſſible!

Gran. Frankly!

Fran. Dear Granger! I did not expect you theſe ten days: how came you to be ſo much better than your word?

Gran. Why, to tell you the truth, becauſe I began to think London better than Paris.

Fran. That's ſtrange: but you never think like other people.

Gran. I am more apt to ſpeak what I think, than other people: though, I confeſs, Paris has its charms; but to me they are like thoſe of a coquette, gay and gaudy; they ſerve to amuſe with, but a man would not chooſe to be married to them. In ſhort, I am to paſs my days in Old England, and am therefore reſolved not to have an ill opinion of it.

Fran. Theſe ſettled thoughts, Ned, make me hope, that if ever you ſhould marry, you will be as partial to the woman you intend to paſs your days with.

Gran. Faith, I think every man's a fool that is not: ' but it's very odd; you ſee, the groſſeſt fools have ge-

A 3   ' nerally

' nerally fenfe enough to be fond of a fine houfe, or a
' fine horfe, when they have bought them : they can fee
' the value of them, at leaft ; and why a poor wife fhould
' not have as fair play for one's inclination, I can fee no
' reafon, but downright ill nature or ftupidity.

' *Fran.* What do you think of avarice ? when people
' purchafe wives, as they do other goods, only becaufe
' they are a pennyworth: then too, a woman has a fine
' time on't.

' *Gran.* Ay, but that will never be the cafe of my
' wife : when I marry, I'll do it with the fame conve-
' nient views as a man would fet up his coach : becaufe
' his eftate will bear it, it's eafy, and keeps him out of
' dirty company.

' *Fran.* But, what! would you have a wife have no
' more charms than a chariot ?

' *Gran.* Ah, friend, if I can but pafs as many eafy
' hours at home with one, as abroad in t'other, I will
' take my chance for her works of fupererogation ; and
' I believe at worft, fhould be upon a par with the hap-
' pinefs of moft hufbands about town.

' *Fran.* But at this rate, you would marry before you
' are in love.

' *Gran.* Why not ? Do you think happinefs is entailed
' upon marrying the woman you love? No more than
' reward is upon public merit: it may give you a title
' to it indeed ; but you muft depend upon other people's
' virtue to find your account in either. For my part, I
' am not for building caftles in the air;' when I marry,
I expect no great matters ; none of your angels, a mortal woman will do my bufinefs, as you'll find, when I
tell you my choice. ' All I defire of a wife, is, that fhe
' will do as fhe is bid, and keep herfelf clean.'

Fran. ' Would you not have her a companion, tho',
' as well as a bedfellow ?

' *Gran.* You mean, I fuppofe, a woman of fenfe.

' *Fran.* I fhould not think it amifs for a man of fenfe.

' *Gran.* Nor I ; but, 's'death ! where fhall I get her ?
' In fhort, I am tired with the fearch, and will ev'n take
' up, with one, as nature has made her, handfome, and
' only a fool of her own making.

4   ' *Fran.*

' *Fran.* Was ever fo defperate an indifference ?' I am impatient till I know her.

Gran. Even the fage and haughty prude, Sophronia.

Fran. Sophronia ! ' I hope you don't take her for a ' fool, Sir :' why, fhe thinks fhe has more fenfe than all her fex together.

Gran. ' You don't tell me that as a proof of her wit, ' I prefume, Sir.

' *Fran.* No: but I think your humour's a little extra-
' ordinary, that can refolve to marry the woman you
' laugh at.

' *Gran.* It's at leaft, a fign I am in no great danger of
- ' her laughing at me, Tom ; the cafe of many a prettier
' fellow. But I take Sophronia to be only a fool of parts,
' that is however capable of thinking right ; and a man
- ' muft be nice indeed, that turns up his nofe at a woman
' who has no worfe imperfection, than fetting too great
' value upon her underftanding.' I grant it fhe is half mad with her learning and philofophy : what then ? fo are moft of our great men, when they get a little too much on't. Nay, fhe is fo rapt in the pride of her ima-
ginary knowledge, that fhe almoft forgets fhe is a wo-
man, and thinks all offers of love to her perfon a dif-
honour to the dignity of her foul ; but all this does not difcourage me : fhe may fancy herfelf as wife as fhe pleafes ; but unlefs I fail in my meafures, I think I fhall have hard luck, if I don't make that fine flefh and blood of hers, as troublefome as my own in a fortnight.

Fran. You muft have better luck than I had then ; I was her fool for above five months together, and did not come ill-recommended to the family ; but could make no more impreffion than upon a veftal virgin ; and *yet*
' how a man of your cool reflexion, can think of at-
' tempting her, I have no notion.

' *Gran.* Pfha! I laugh at all her airs : a woman of
' a general infenfibility, is only one that has never been
' rightly attacked.

' *Fran.* Are you then really refolved to purfue her ?

' *Gran.* Why not ? Is not fhe a fine creature ? Has
' not fhe parts ? Would not half her knowledge, equally
' divided, make fifty coquettes all women of fenfe ? Is

' not

' not her beauty natural, her perfon lovely, her mien
' majeftic?——Then fuch a conftitution——

'*Fran.* Nay, fhe has a wholefome look, I grant you:
' but then her prudery, and Platonic principles, are in-
' fupportable.

'*Gran.* Now to me they are more diverting, than all
' the levity of a coquette: Oh, the noble conflicts be-
' tween nature and a proud underftanding, make our tri-
' umphs fo infinitely above thofe petty conquefts——
' Befides, are not you philofopher enough to know, my
' friend, that a body continent holds moft of the thing
' contained? 'Tis not your wafting current, but refer-
' voirs, that make the fountain play; not the prodigal's,
' but the mifer's cheft that holds the treafure. No, no,
' take my word, your prude has thrice the latent fire of
' a coquette. Your prude's flafk hermetically fealed, all's
' right within, depend upon't; but your coquette's a
' mere bottle of plague-water, that's open to every
' body.

'*Fran.* Well, Sir, fince you feem fo heartily in earneft,
' and, I fee, are not to be difgufted at a little female
' frailty: I think I ought in honour to let you into a
' little more of her. You muft know then,' this marble-
hearted lady, who could not bear my addreffes to herfelf,
has, notwithftanding, flefh and blood enough to be con-
foundedly uneafy, that I now pay them to her fifter.

Gran. I am glad to hear it. Pr'ythee, let me know
all; for 'tis upon thefe fort of weakneffes that I am to
ftrengthen my hopes.

'*Fran.* You know, I writ you word, that I thought the
' fafeft way to convey my real paffion for her fifter Char-
' lotte, would be to drop my cold pretenfions to Sophro-
' nia infenfibly; upon which account I rather heightened
' my refpect to her: but as, you know, 'tis harder to
' difguife a real inclination, than to diffemble one we
' have not; Sophronia, it feems, has fo far fufpected the
' cheat, that, fince your abfence, fhe has broke into a
' thoufand little impatiences at my new happinefs with
' Charlotte.

'*Gran.* Good.'

Fran. But the jeft is, fhe can't yet bring down her vanity to believe I am in earneft with Charlotte neither;
but

but really fancies my addresses there are all grimace ; the mere malice of a rejected lover, to give her scorn a jealousy.

Gran. Admirable ! ' but I hope you are sure of this.

' *Fran.* 'Twas but yesterday she gave me a proof of it.

' *Gran.* Pray, let's hear.

' *Fran.* Why, as Charlotte and I were whispering at
' one end of a room, while we thought her wrapt up in
' one of Horace's odes at the other, of a sudden I observed
' her come sailing up to me, with an insulting smile, as
' who should say—I laugh at all these shallow arts——
' then turned short, and looking over her shoulder, cried
' aloud,——*Ah, miser !*

' *Quantâ laboras in Charybdi !*

' *Gran. Digne puer meliore flammâ*——Ah! methinks
' I see the imperious hussy in profile, waving her snowy
' neck into a thousand lovely attitudes of scorn and tri-
' umph ! Oh, the dear vanity !' Well, when all's said,
the coxcomb's vastly handsome.

' *Fran.* 'Egad, thou art the oddest fellow in the world,
' to be thus capable of diverting yourself with your mis-
' tress's jealousy of another man.

' *Gran.* Psha ! Thou'rt too refined a lover ; I am
' glad of any occasion that proves her more a woman
' than she imagines.

' *Fran.* But pray, Sir, upon what foot did you stand
' with her before you went to France ?

' *Gran.* Oh, I never pretended to more than a Platonic
' passion ; I saw, at first view, she was inaccessible by
' love.

' *Fran.* Yet, since you were resolved to pursue her,
' how came you to think of rambling to Paris ?

' *Gran.* Why, the last time I saw her, she grew so fan-
' tastically jealous of my regarding her more as a woman,
' than an intellectual being, that my patience was half
' tired ; and having, at that time, an appointment with
' some idle company to make a trip to Paris, I slily took
' that occasion, and told her, if I threw myself into a
' voluntary banishment from her person, I hoped she
' would then be convinced, I had no other views of hap-
' piness, than what her letters might, even in absence,
' as well gratify, from the charms of her understanding.

' *Fran.*

' *Fran.* Moſt ſolemnly impudent.

' *Gran.* In ſhort, her vanity was ſo blind to the ban-
' ter, that ſhe infiſted upon my going, and made me a con-
' ditional promiſe of anſwering all my letters ; in which
' I have flattered her romantic folly to that degree, that in
' her laſt, ſhe confeſſes an entire ſatisfaction in the Inno-
' cent Dignity of my inclinations (as ſhe ſtiles it) and
' therefore thinks herſelf bound in gratitude to recall me
' from exile : which gracious boon (being heartily tired
' at Paris) I am now arrived to accept of.

' *Fran.* The merrieſt amour that ever was ! Well,'
and, *Frank*, why don't you viſit her ?

Gran. Oh ! I do all things by rule—not till ſhe has di-
ned ; for our great Engliſh philoſopher, my Lord Bacon,
tells you, that then the mind is generally moſt ductile.

Fran. Wiſely confidered.

Gran. Beſides, I want to have a little talk firſt with the
old gentleman her father.

Fran. Sir Gilbert ! If I don't miſtake, yonder he comes.

Gran. Where, pr'ythee ?

Fran. There, by the bookſeller's ; don't you ſee him,
with an odd crowd after him ?

Gran. Oh ! now I have him——he's loaded with pa-
pers, like a ſolicitor.

Fran. Sir, he is, at this time, a man of the firſt conſe-
quence, and receives more petitions every hour, than the
court of chancery in a whole term.

Gran. What ! is he lord treaſurer ?

Fran. A much more confiderable perſon, I can aſſure
you ; he is a South Sea director, Sir.

Gran. Oh, I cry you mercy ! and thoſe about him, I
preſume, are bowing for ſubſcriptions.

Fran. That's their buſineſs, you may be ſure ; but ſee,
at laſt he has broke from them. *Let's*

' *Gran.* No : there's one has got him by the ſleeve
' again.'

Fran. ' What if we ſhould ' ſtand off, and obſerve a
little ?

Gran. With all my heart.

Sir Gilb. [*To a Man at the door.*] Pr'ythee, be, quiet,
fellow ! I tell you I'll ſend the Duke an anſwer to-mor-
row morning.

[Within.

[*Within.*] It's very well, Sir——

Sir Gilbert *speaks, entering with a great parcel of open
-letters in his hand, and others stuffing his pockets.*

Sir Gilb. Very well ! aye, so it is, if he gets it then—
Why ! what ! these people of quality, sure, think they
do you a favour when they ask one—Huh, let him come
for it himself ! I am sure I was forced to do so at his
house, when I came for my own, and could not get it neither—and he expects I should give him two thousand
pounds only for sending a footman to me. Why ! what !
Does his Grace think I don't know which side my bread's
buttered on ? Let's see ! ' who are these from ? [*Reads*
' *to himself.*

' *Gran.* The old gentleman's no blind admirer of a
' man of quality, I see.

' *Fran.* Oh, Sir ! he has lately taken up a mortal aver-
' sion to any man that has a better title than himself.

' *Gran.* How so pray ?

' *Fran.* As he grows rich, he grows proud ; and among
' friends, had lately a mind to be made a lord himself ;
' but applying to the wrong person, it seems he was dis-
' appointed ; and ever since piques himself upon despi-
' sing any nobleman who is not as rich as himself.

' *Gran.* Hah ! the right plebeian spirit of Old Eng-
' land : but I think he's counted an honest man.

' *Fran.* Umph ! Yes, well enough—a good sort of a
' mercantile conscience : he is punctual in bargains, and
' expects the same from others ; he will neither steal nor
' cheat, unless he thinks he has the protection of the law :
' then indeed, as most thriving men do, he thinks ho-
' nour and equity are chimerical notions.

' *Gran.* That is, he bluntly professes what other peo-
' ple practise with more breeding—But let's accost him.

' *Fran.* Stay a little.

' *Enter a Footman, with a Letter.*

' *Sir Gilb.* To me, friend !——What, will they never
' have done ?

' *Footm.* Sir, my Lady Double-chin presents her ser-
' vice, and says she'll call for your honour's answer to-
' morrow morning.

Sir

' *Sir Gilb.* Very well ; tell my Lady, I'll take care—
' [*Exit Footman.*] to be exactly out of the way when she
' comes.

' *Gran.* Hah ! he'll keep that part of his word, I war-
' rant him.

' *Sir Gilb.* Let's fee : the old story, I suppofe—[*Reads.*]
' Um—um—yes, yes—only two thoufand—Hah ! does
' the woman take me for a fool ? Does she think I don't
' know, that a two thoufand fubfcription is worth two
' thoufand guineas ? And becaufe she is not worth above
' fourfcore thoufand already, she would have me give
' them to her for nothing. To a poor relation, she pre-
' tends, indeed ; as if she loved any body better than
' herfelf. A drum ! and a fiddle ! I'll greafe none of
' your fat fows, not I.'—No, no ; get you into the ne-
gative pocket—— Blefs my eyes ! Mr. Granger !

Gran. Sir Gilbert, I am your moft humble fervant.

Sir Gilb. In troth, I am glad to fee you in England
again—Mr. Frankly, your humble fervant.

Fran. Sir, your moft obedient.

Sir Gilb. Well, how goes Miffiffippi, man ? What, do
they bring their money by waggon loads to market ftill ?
Hay ! ha, ha, ha !

Gran. Oh, all gone ! Good for nothing, Sir ! Your
South Sea has brought it to wafte paper.

Sir Gilb. Why, ay, han't we done glorious things here,
ha ? We have found work for the coachmakers as well as
they, boy.

Gran. Ah, Sir, in a little time we shall reduce thofe,
who kept them there, to their original of riding behind
them here.

Sir Gilb. Huh, huh ! you will have your joke ftill, I
fee——Well, you have not fold out, I hope.

Gran. Not I, faith, Sir ; the old five thoufand lies fnug
as it was. I don't fee where one can move it and mend
it ; fo e'en let it lie, and breed by itfelf.

Sir Gilb. You're right, you're right——hark you—
keep it—the thing will do more ftill, boy.

Gran. Sir, I am fure it's in hands that can make it do
any thing.

Sir Gilb. Have you got any new fubfcriptions ?

Gran. You know, Sir, I have been abfent ; and it is
really

really now grown fo valuable a favour, I have not the confidence to afk it.

Sir Gilb. Pfha ! pr'ythee, never talk of that, man.

Gran. If I thought you were not full, Sir ——

Sir Gilb. Why, if I were as full as a bumper, Sir, I'll put my friends in, let who will run over for it.

Fran. Sir Gilbert always doubles his favours by his manner of doing them.

Sir Gilb. Frankly, you are down for five thoufand pounds already, and you may depend upon every fhilling of it—Let me fee—what have I done with my lift ?—— Granger has a good eftate, and had an eye upon my eldeft daughter before he went to France. I muft have him in ; it may chance to bring the matter to bear. [*Afide.*

Gran. Where did you get all thefe letters, Sir Gilbert ?

Sir Gilb. Why, ay, this is the trade every morning ; all for fubfcriptions. Nay, they are fpecial ftuff—Here, pr'ythee, read that.

Fran. Who is it from, Sir ?

Sir Gilb. Oh, a North-Briton ! a bloody, fquabbling fellow, who owes me a thoufand pounds for difference, and that's his way of paying me. Read it.

Gran. [*Reading.*] " Wuns, Sir, de ye no tack me for a man of honour ! Ye need no fend to my ludging fo often for year pimping thoufand pound. An ye'll be but civil a bit, Ife order the bearer, my brocker, to mack up year balance ; an if ye wull but gee yourfel the trouble to put his name intull your own lift for a thoufand fubfcription, he'fe pay ye aw down upo' the nail : but an ye wunna do this fmaw jubb, the deel dom me an ye e'er fee a groat from me, as long as my name is

George Blunderbufs."

Fran. What can you do with fuch a fellow, Sir ?

Sir Gilb. Do with him ! why, I'll let him have it, and get my money. I had better do that, than be obliged to fight for it, or give it to the lawyers.

Fran. Nay, that's true too.

Sir Gilb. Here's another, now, from one of my wife's hopeful relations ; an extravagant puppy, that has rattled a gilt chariot to pieces before it was paid for. But he'll die in jail.

Fran.

Fran. [*Reading.*]——" Dear knight."——I fee he is familiar.

Sir Gilb. Nay, it's all of a piece.

Fran. [*Reading.*] " Not to mince the matter ; yefter-day, at Marybone, they had me all bob as a Robin. In fhort, being out of my money, I was forced to come the cafter, and tumbled for five hundred, dead : befides which, I owe Crop, the lender, a brace ; and if I have a fingle Si-mon to pay him, rot me. But the queer coll promifes to advance me t'other three, and bring me home, provided you will let him fneak into your lift for a cool thoufand. You know it's a debt of honour in me, and will coft you nothing.   Yours in hafte,
                                 Robert Rattle."

Fran. The ftile is extraordinary.

Gran. And his motives irrefiftible.

Sir Gilb. Nay, I have them from all nations ; here's one now from an Irifh relation of my own.

Fran. Oh ! pray, let's fee.

Sir Gilb. There.   [Frankly *reads.*

" Loving coufin, and my dear life.

" There is only my brother Patrick, and dat is two of us ; and becaufe we would have a great refpect for our relations, we are come poft from Tipperary, with a loving defign to put both our families upon one anoder. And though we have no acquaintance with your brave daugh-ters, we faw them yefterday at the cathedral church, and find they vil fharve us vel enough. And to fhew our fincere affections, we vil taak dem vidout never a penny of money ; only, as a fmall token of fhivility upon your fide, we defire the faavour of both of us each ten thou-fand in this fame new fubfcription. And becaufe, in our hafte, fome of our cloaths and bills of exchange were for-got, prydee be fo grateful as to fend us two fcore pounds, to put us into fome worfhip for the mean time. So dis was all from, my dear life,
                        Your humble farvant,
                          And loving relation,
                            Owen Mac Ogle."

Fran. A very modeft epiftle, truly !

Sir Gilb. Oh, here's my lift——Now, Mr. Granger, we'll fee what we can do for you. Hold, here are fome
                                              people

people that have no bufinefs here, I am fure—ay, here is
Dr. Bullanbear, one thoufand—Why, ay, I was forced
to put him down to get rid of him. The man has no
confcience. Don't I know he's in every court-lift under
a fham name? Indeed, Domine Doctor, you can't be
here. [*Scratches him out.*] Then here's another favourite
of my wife's too; Signor Caponi da Capo—two thoufand—What, becaufe he can get as much for a fong, does
he think to have it for whiftling too?—Huh, huh, huh!
not I, troth; I am not for fending our money into popifh
countries.   [*Blots him out.*

Fran. Rightly confidered, Sir.

Sir Gilb. Let's fee who's next——' Sir James Baker,
' Knt. one thoufand.

' *Gran.* Who's he, Sir?

' *Sir Gilb.* Oh, a very ingenious perfon! he's well
' known at court; he muft ftand; befides, I believe we
' fhall employ him in our Spanifh trade——Oh! here
' we can you fpare one, I believe—Sir Ifaac Bickerftaff,
' Knt. one thoufand.

' *Fran.* What, the fam'd cenfor of Great Britain?

' *Sir Gilb.* No, no, he was a very honeft, pleafant fel-
' low; this is only a relation, a mere whimfical, that
' will draw nobody's way but his own, and is always
' wifer than his betters. I don't underftand that fort of
' wifdom, that's for doing good to every body but him-
' felf. Let thofe lift him that like him; he fhall ride in
' no troop of mine, odfheartlikins!   [*Blots him.*
' *Gran.* How he damns them with a dafh, like a pro-
' fcribing triumvir!

' *Sir Gilb.* Let's fee.'—I would fain have another for
you——Oh, here! William Penkethman, one thoufand.
Ha, a very pretty fellow, truly! What, give a thoufand
pounds to a player! why, it's enough to turn his brain:
we fhall have him grow proud, and quit the ftage upon it.
No, no, keep him poor, and let him mind his bufinefs;
if the puppy leaves off playing the fool, he's undone.
No, no, I won't hurt the ftage; my wife loves plays, and
whenever fhe is there, I am fure of three hours quiet at
home—[*Blots, &c.*]—Let's fee; one, three, four, five;
ay, juft Frankly's fum—Here's five thoufand for you,
Mr. Granger, with a wet finger.

Gran. Sir, I fhall ever be in your debt.

Sir Gilb. Pooh ! you owe me nothing.

Fran. You have the happinefs of this life, Sir Gilbert, the power of obliging all about you.

Sir Gilb. Oh, Mr. Frankly, money won't do every thing ! I am uneafy at home for all this.

Fran. Is that poffible, Sir, while you have fo fine a lady ?

Sir Gilb. Ay, ay, you are her favourite, and have learning enough to underftand her; but fhe is too wife and too wilful for me.

Fran. Oh, Sir! learning's a fine accomplifhment in a fine lady.

Sir Gilb. Ay, it's no matter for that, fhe's a great plague to me. Not but my lord bifhop, her uncle, was a mighty good man; fhe lived all along with him; I took her upon his word; 'twas he made her a fcholar; I thought her a miracle; before I had her, I ufed to go and hear her talk Latin with him an hour together; and there I—I—I played the fool——I was wrong, I was wrong—I fhould not have married again—and yet, I was fo fond of her parts, I begged him to give my eldeft daughter the fame fine education; and fo he did—but, to tell you the truth, I believe both their heads are turned.

Gran. A good hufband, Sir, would fet your daughter right, I warrant you.

Sir G. He muft come out of the clouds, then; for fhe thinks no mortal man can deferve her. What think you, Mr. Frankly, you had foon enough of her ?

Fran. I think ftill, fhe may deferve any mortal man, Sir.

Gran. I can't boaft of my merit, Sir Gilbert; but I wifh you would give me leave to take my chance with her.

Sir Gilb. Will you dine with me ?

Gran. Sir, you fhall not afk me twice.

Sir Gilb. And you, Mr. Frankly ?

Fran. Thank you, Sir ; I have had the honour of my Lady's invitation before I came out.

Sir Gilb. Oh, then, pray don't fail ; for when you are there, fhe is always in humour.

Gran. I hope, Sir, we fhall have the happinefs of the young lady's company too.

Sir

Sir Gilb. Ay, ay, after dinner I'll talk with you.

Fran. Not forgetting your favourite, Charlotte, Sir.

Sir Gilb. Look you, Mr. Frankly, I underſtand you ; you have a mind to my daughter Charlotte, and I have often told you I have no exceptions to you ; and there-fore you may well wonder why I yet ſcruple my conſent.

Fran. You have a right to refuſe it, no doubt, Sir ; but I hope you can't blame me for aſking it.

Sir Gilb. In troth, I don't ; and I wiſh you had it, with all my heart. But ſo it is—there's no comfort, ſure, in this life ; for, though, by this glorious ſtate of our ſtocks, I have raiſed my poor ſingle plumb to a pomgra-nate, yet if they had not riſen quite ſo high, you and I, Mr. Frankly, might poſſibly have been both happier men than we are.

Fran. How ſo, Sir ?

Sir Gilb. Why, at the price it now is, I am under con-tract to give one of the greateſt coxcombs upon earth the refuſal of marrying which of my daughters he pleaſes.

Gran. Hey-day ! What, is marriage a bubble too ?
                                                    [*Aſide.*

Sir Gilb. Nay, and am bound in honour even to ſpeak a good word for him. You know young Witling.

Fran. I could have gueſs'd your coxcomb, Sir ; but I hope he has not yet named the lady.

Sir Gilb. Not directly ; but I gueſs his inclinations, and expect every hour to have him make his call upon my conſent according to form.

' *Fran.* Is this poſſible ?

Gran. Sir, if he ſhould happen to name Sophronia, will you give me leave to drub him out of his contract ?

Sir Gilb. By no means ; credit's a nice point, and peo-ple won't ſuppoſe that would be done without my conni-vance : ' beſide, I believe Sophronia's in no danger. But ' becauſe one can be ſure of nothing, gentlemen, I de-' mand both your words of honour, that, for my ſake, ' you will neither of you uſe any acts of hoſtility.

' *Fran.* Sir, in this caſe, you have a right to com-' mand us.

' *Sir Gilb.* Your hands upon't.

' *Both.* And our words of honour.

' *Sir Gilb.* I am ſatisfied'—If we can find a way to out-

wit

wit him, fo; if not—Odfo! here he comes—I beg your
pardon, gentlemen; but I won't be in his way, till I cannot help it. Hum, hum!   [*Exit* Sir Gilb.

Gran. A very odd circumftance.

Fran. I am afraid there's fomething in it; and begin
to think, now, my friend, Witling, (in his raillery yefter-
day with Charlotte) knew what he faid himfelf, tho' he
did not care whether any body elfe did.

Gran. Sure it cannot be real! I always took Witling
for a beggar.

Fran. So he was, or very near it, fome months ago;
but fince fortune has been playing her tricks here, fhe has
rewarded his merit, it feems, with about an hundred thoufand pounds out of Change-alley.

Gran. Nay, then he may be dangerous indeed.

Fran. I long to know the bottom of it.

Gran. That you can't fail of; for you know he is vain
and familiar—and here he comes.

                 Enter Witling.

Wit. Ha, my little Granger! how doft thou do, child?
Where the devil haft thou been this age? What's the reafon you never come among us? Frankly, give me thy
little finger, my dear.

Gran. Thou art a very impudent fellow, Witling.

Wit. Ay, it's no matter for that; thou art a pleafant
one, I am fure; for thou always makeft us laugh.

Fran. Us! What the devil doft thou mean by us, now?

Wit. Why, your pretty fellows, my dear; your *bons
vivants*; your men of wit and tafte, child.

Gran. I know very few of thofe; but I come from a
country, Sir, where half the nation are juft fuch pretty
fellows as thou art.

Wit. Ha! that muft be a pleafant place indeed! What,
doft thou come from Paradife, child? Ha, ha, ha!

' *Fran.* Don't you know he is juft come from France,
' Sir?

' *Wit.* You jeft!

' *Gran.* Why, ay—Now you fee, Witling, your vani-
' ty has brought you into a fool's Paradife.

' *Wit.* Oh, you pleafant cur! What, Paris, *quafi par
' diis*, or Paradife. Ha! I wifh I had been with you: I
' am fure you would have thought it Paradife then.

                3   ' *Gran.*

' *Gran.* Nay, now he's fairly in.

' *Wit.* 'Tis impoffible to be out on't, Sir, in your com-
' pany ; wherever you are, it is always Paradife to me,
' depend upon't. Ha, ha!'

Fran. Faith, Granger, there I think he came up with
you.

Gran. Nay, fince the rogue has money, we muft, of
courfe, allow him wit: but I think he is one of your
good-natur'd ones; he does not only find the jeft, but
the laugh too.

Wit. Ay, and to hear thee talk, child, how is it poffible to want either? Ha, ha!

Fran. Good again! Well faid, Witling! Why, thou
art as fharp to-day——

Wit. As a glover's needle, my dear; I always dart it
into your leather heads with three edges, ha, ha!

Gran. Pr'ythee, Witling, does not thy affurance fometimes meet with a repartee that only lights upon the out-
fide of thy head?

Wit. Oh, your fervant, Sir! What, now your fire's
gone, you would knock me down with the butt-end,
would you? Ha! it's very well, Sir; I ha' done, Sir, I
ha' done; I fee it's a folly to draw bills upon a man that
has no affets.

Gran. And to do it upon a man that has no cafh o'
thine in his hands, is the impudence of a bankrupt.

Wit. Pfha! a mere flafh in the pan—' Well, well, it's
' all over'—Come, come, a truce, a truce; I have done;
I beg pardon.

' *Gran.* Why, thou vain rogue, thy good-nature has
' more impudence than thy wit. Doft thou fuppofe I
' can ever take any thing ill of thee.

' *Wit.* Pfha! fie! what doft thou talk, man? Why,
' I know thou canft not live without me. Doft think I
' don't know how to make allowances? Tho' if I have
' too much wit, and thou haft too little, how the devil
' can either of us help it, you know? Ha, ha!

' *Fran.* Ha, ha! honeft Witling is not to be put out
' of humour, I fee.

' *Gran.* No, faith, nor out of countenance——

' *Wit.* Not I, faith, my friend; and a man of turn
' may fay any thing to me—Not but I fee by his hu-
' mour,

'mour, fomething has gone wrong—I hold fix to four,
' now, thou haft been crabbed at Paris in the Miffiffippi.

' *Gran.* Not I, faith, Sir; I would no more put my
' money into the ftocks there, than my legs into the ftocks
' here. There's no getting home again, when you have
' a mind to it.

' *Wit.* Ha! very good. But, pr'ythee, tell us; what;
' is the Quinquinpois as pleafant as our Change-alley
' here?

' *Gran.* Much the fame comedy, Sir, where poor wife
' men are only fpectators, and laugh to fee fools make
' their fortune.

' *Wit.* Ay, but there we differ, Sir; for there are men
' of wit too, that have made their fortunes among us, to
' my knowledge.

' *Gran.* Very likely, Sir; when fools are flufh of mo-
' ney, men of wit won't be long without it. I hear you
' have been fortunate, Sir.

' *Wit.* Humh—'Egad I don't know whether he calls
' me a wit or a fool.

' *Gran.* Oh, fie! every body knows you have a great
' deal of money.

' *Fran.* And I don't know any man pretends to more
' wit.

' *Wit.* Nay, that's true too: but—'Egad, I believe he
' has me.'

Gran. But, pr'ythee, Witling, how came a man of thy
parts ever to think of raifing thy fortune in Change-alley? How didft thou make all this money thou art mafter of?

Wit. Why, as other men of wit and parts often do, by
having little or nothing to lofe. I raifed my fortune,
Sir, as Milo lifted the bull, by fticking to it every day,
when 'twas but a calf. I foufed them with premiums,
child, and laid them on thick when the ftock was low;
and did it all from a brafs nail, boy. In fhort, by being
dirty once a day for a few months, taking a lodging at
my broker's, and rifing at the fame hour I ufed to go to
bed at this end of the town. I have at laft made up my
accounts, and now wake every morning mafter of five-
and-twenty hundred a year, *terra firma*, and pelf in my
ocket: I have fun in my fob, befide, child.

Gran.

Gran. And all this out of Change-alley ?

Wit. Every shilling, Sir; all out of stocks, puts, bulls, rams, bears, and bubbles.

' *Gran.* These frolicks of Fortune do some justice at
' least; they sufficiently mortify the proud and envious,
' that have not been the better for them.

' *Fran.* Oh, I know some are ready to burst even at
' the good fortune of their own relations !

' *Wit.* 'Egad, and so do I; there's that surly put, my
' uncle, the counsellor, won't pull off his hat to me now.
' A poor slaving cur, that is not worth above a thousand
' a year, and minds nothing but his business——

' *Fran.* And so is out of humour with you, because you
' have done that in a twelvemonth, that he has been
' drudging for these twenty years.

' *Wit.* But I intend to send him word, if he does not
' mend his manners now, I shall disinherit him.'

Gran. What are we to think of this, Frankly ? Is Fortune really in her wits, or is the world out of them?

Fran. Much as it used to be; she has only found a new channel for her tides of favour.

Wit. Pr'ythee, why dost not come into the Alley, and see us scramble for them ? If you have a mind to philosophize there, there's work for your speculation ! 'Egad, I never go there, but it puts me in mind of the poetical regions of death, where all mankind are upon a level:
' there you'll see a duke dangling after a director; here
' a peer and a 'prentice haggling for an eighth; there a
' Jew and a parson making up differences; here a young
' woman of quality buying bears of a quaker; and there
' an old one selling refusals to a lieutenant of grenadiers.

' *Frank.* What a medley of mortals has he jumbled
' together !'

' *Wit.*' Oh, there's no such fun in the universe !——
'Egad, there's no getting away. Perish me, if I've had time to see my mistress, but of a Sunday, these three months.

Gran. Thy mistress ! What dost thou mean ? Thou speakest as if thou hadst but one.

Wit. Why, no more I have not, that I care a farthing for : I may perhaps have a stable of scrubs, to mount my
footmen

footmen, when I rattle into town, or fo ; but this is a choice pad, child, that I defign for my own riding.

Frank. Pr'ythee, who is fhe ?

Wit. I'll fhew you, my dear——I think I have her here in my pocket.

Gran. What doft thou mean ?

Wit. Look you, I know you are my friends ; and there-fore fince I am fure it is in nobody's power to hurt me, I'll venture to truft you.——There ! that's whoo, child.

[*Shews a Paper.*

Fran. What's here ?   [*Reads.*

" To Sir GILBERT WRANGLE.

" Sir, according to your contract of the 11th of February laft, I now make my election of your younger daughter, Mrs. Charlotte Wrangle ; and do hereby demand your confent, to be forthwith join'd to the faid Charlotte in the fober ftate of matrimony.   Witnefs my hand, &c.

WILLIAM WITLING."

Fran. What a merry world do we live in !

Gran. This indeed is extraordinary.

Wit. I think fo : I affure you, gentlemen, I take this to be a *coup de maître* of the whole Alley.   This is a call now, that none of your thick-fculled calculators could ever have thought on.

Gran. Well, Sir, and does this contract fecure the la-dy's fortune to you too ?

Wit. Oh, pox ! I knew that was all rug before : he had fettled three thoufand a-piece upon them in the South Sea, when it was only about par, provided they married with his confent, which by this contract, you know, I have a right to.   So there's another thirty thou-fand dead, my dear.

Fran. But pray, Sir, has not the lady herfelf a right of refufal, as well as you, all this while ?

Wit. A right ! aye, who doubts it ? Every woman has a right to be a fool, if fhe has a mind to it, that's certain : but Charlotte happens to be a girl of tafte, my dear ; fhe is none of thofe fools that will ftand in her own light, I can tell you.

Fran. Well, but do you expect fhe fhould blindly con-fent to your bargain ?

Wit. Blindly, no, child : but doft thou imagine any citizen's citizen's daughter can refuse a man of my figure and fortune, with her eyes open?

Gran. Impudent rogue! [*Aside.*

Fran. Nay, I grant, your security's good, Sir: but I mean, you have still left her consent at large in the writing.

Wit. Her consent! Didſt thou think I minded that, man? I knew, if the ſtock did but whip up, I ſhould make no more of her than a poached egg. But to let you into the ſecret, my dear, I am ſecure of that already; for the ſlut's in love with me, and does not know it: ha, ha, ha!

Fran. How came you to know it then?

Wit. By her ridiculous pretending to hate me, child: for we never meet, but 'tis a mortal war, and never part, till one of us is rallied to death: ha, ha, ha!

Fran. Nay then, it muſt be a match; for, I ſee, you are reſolved to take no anſwer.

Wit. Not I, faith! I know her play too well for that: in ſhort, I am this very evening to attack her in form; and to ſhew you I am a man of ſkill, I intend to make my firſt breach from a battery of Italian muſic, in which I deſign to ſing my own Io Pæan, and enter the town in triumph.

Fran. You are not going to her now?

Wit. No, no, I muſt firſt go and give the governor my ſummons here. I muſt find out Sir Gilbert; he's hereabouts: I long to make him growl a little; for I know he'll fire when he reads it, as if it were a *ſcire facias* againſt the company's charter. Ha, ha, ha! [*Exit* Wit.

' *Fran.* When all's ſaid, this fellow ſeems to feel his ' fortune more than moſt of the fools that have been ' lately taken into her favour.'

Gran. ' Pox on him! I had rather have his conſtitu-' tion than his money.' Pr'ythee let's follow, and ſee how the old gentleman receives him.

Fran. No; excuſe me; I can't reſt till I ſee Charlotte: you know, my affairs now require attendance.

Gran. That's true; I beg you take no notice to Sophronia of my being in town; I have my reaſons for it.

Fran. Very well; we ſhall meet at dinner. Adieu.

[*Exeunt ſeverally.*

END of the FIRST ACT.

ACT

ACT II.

SCENE, *Sir* Gilbert's *House.*

Sophronia *and* Charlotte.

CHARLOTTE.

HA, ha, ha !

Soph. Dear fifter, don't be fo boifterous in your mirth : you really over-power me ! So much vocifera-tion is infupportable.

Char. Well, well, I beg your pardon—but, you know laughing is the wholfomeft thing in the world; and when one has a hearty occafion——

Soph. To be vulgar, you are refolved to appear fo.

Char. Oh, I cannot help it, I love you dearly ; and, pray, where's the harm of it ?

Soph. Look you, fifter, I grant you, that rifibility is only given to the *animal rationale* ; but you really in-dulge it, as if you could give no other proof of your fpe-cies.

Char. And if I were to come into your fentiments, dear fifter, I am afraid the world would think I were of no fpecies at all.

Soph. The world, fifter, is a generation of ignorants : and, for my part, I am refolved to do what in me lies, to put an end to pofterity.

Char. Why, you don't defpair of a man, I hope !

Soph. No ; but I will have all mankind defpair of me.

Char. You'll pofitively die a maid ?

Soph. You, perhaps, may think that dying a martyr ; but I fhall not die a brute, depend upon't.

Char. Nay, I don't think you'll die either, if you can help it.

Soph. What do you mean, Madam ?

Char. Only, Madam, that you are a woman, and may happen to change your mind ; that's all.

Soph. A woman ! That's fo like your ordinary way of thinking ; as if fouls had any fexes—No—when I die, Madam, I fhall endeavour to leave fuch fentiments be-hind me, that—*(non omnis moriar)* the world will be con-vinced my purer part had no fex at all.

' *Char.*

' *Char.* Why truly, it will be hard to imagine, that
' any one of our fex could make fuch a refolution;
' though, I hope, we are not bound to keep all we make
' neither.

' *Soph.* You'll find, Madam, that an elevated foul may
' be always mafter of its perifhable part.'

Char. But, dear Madam, do you fuppofe our fouls are
crammed into our bodies merely to fpoil fport, that a
virtuous woman is only fent hither of a fool's errand?
What's the ufe of our coming into the world, if we are to
go out of it, and leave nobody behind us?

Soph. ' If our fpecies can be only fupported by thofe
' grofs mixtures, of which cookmaids and footmen are
' capable, people of rank and erudition ought certainly
' to deteft them.' Oh, what a pity 'tis the divine fecret
fhould be loft! I have fomewhere read of an ancient na-
turalift, whofe laborious ftudies had difcovered a more
innocent way of propagation; but, it feems, his tables
unfortunately falling into his wife's hands, the grofs
creature threw them into the fire.

Char. Indeed, my dear fifter, if you talk thus in company, people will take you for a mad-woman.

' *Soph.* I fhall be even with them, and think thofe mad,
' that differ from my opinion.

' *Char.* But I rather hope the world will be fo chari-
' table, as to think this is not your real opinion.'

Soph. I fhall wonder at nothing that's faid or thought
by people of your fullied imagination.

Char. Sullied! I would have you to know, Madam, I
think of nothing but what's decent and natural.

Soph. Don't be too pofitive, nature has it indecencies.

Char. That may be; but I don't think of them.

Soph. No! Did not you own to me juft now, you were
determined to marry?

Char. Well; and where's the crime, pray?

Soph. What! you want to have me explain? But I
fhall not defile my imagination with fuch grofs ideas.

' *Char.* But, dear Madam, if marriage were fuch an
' abominable bufinefs, how comes it that all the world
' allows it to be honourable? And I hope you won't ex-
' pect me to be wifer than any of my anceftors, by think-
' ing the contrary.

' *Soph.*

' *Soph.* No; but if you will read hiftory, fifter, you
' will find that the fubjects of the greateft empire upon
' earth were only propagated from violated chaftity:
' the Sabine ladies were wives, 'tis true, but glorious
' ravifhed wives. Vanquifhed they were indeed, but
' they furrendered not : they fcreamed, and cried, and
' tore, and as far as their weak limbs would give them
' leave, refifted and abhorred the odious joy——

' *Char.* And yet, for all that nicenefs, they brought
' a chopping race of rakes, that bullied the whole world
' about them.

' *Soph.* The greater ftill their glory, that though they
' were naturally prolific, their refiftance proved they
' were not flaves to appetite.

' *Char.* Ah, fifter! if the Romans had not been fo
' fharp fet, the glorious refiftance of thefe fine ladies
' might have been all turned into coquettry.

' *Soph.* There's the fecret, fifter: had our modern
' dames but the true Sabine fpirit of difdain, mankind
' might be again reduced to thofe old Roman extremi-
' ties; and our fhamelefs brides would not then be led,
' but dragged to the altar; their *fponfalia* not called a
' marriage, but a facrifice : and the conquered beauty,
' not the bridal virgin, but the victim.

' *Char.* Oh, ridiculous! and fo you would have no
' woman married, that was not firft ravifhed, according
' to law ?

' *Soph.* I would have mankind owe their conqueft of
' us rather to the weaknefs of our limbs, than of our
' fouls. And if defencelefs women muft be mothers, the
' brutality, at leaft, fhould lie all at their door.'

Char. Have a care of this over-nicenefs, dear fifter,
left fome agreeable young fellow fhould feduce you to
the confufion of parting with it. You'd make a moft
rueful figure in love !

Soph. Sifter, you make me fhudder at your freedom !
I in love! I admit a man! What, become the voluntary, the lawful object of a corporeal fenfuality ! Like
you, to choofe myfelf a tyrant! a defpoiler ! a hufband !
Ugh.

Char. I am afraid, by this diforder of your thoughts,
dear

dear fifter, you have got one in your head, that you don't know how to get rid of.

Soph. I have, indeed; but it's only the male creature that you have a mind to.

Char. Why, that's poffible too; for I have often obferved you uneafy at Mr. Frankly's being particular to me.

Soph. If I am, 'tis upon your account, becaufe I know he impofes upon you.

Char. You know it?

' *Soph.* I know his heart, and that another is miftrefs
' of it.

' *Char.* Another!

' *Soph.* Another; but one that to my knowledge will
' never hear of him; fo don't be uneafy, dear fifter, all'
' in my power you may be affured of.

' *Char.* Surprifingly kind, indeed!

' *Soph.* And you know too I have a great deal in my
' inclination ———

' *Char.* For me or him, dear fifter?

' *Soph.* Nay, now you won't fuffer me to oblige you;
' I tell you, I hate the animal; and for half a good word
' would give him away.

' *Char.* What! before you have him?

' *Soph.* This affected ignorance is fo vain, dear fifter,
' that I now think it high time to explain to you.

' *Char.* Then we fhall underftand one another.'

Soph. You don't know, perhaps, that Mr. Frankly is paffionately in love with me?

Char. I know, upon his treating with my father, his lawyer once made you fome offers.

Soph. Why then you may know too, that upon my flighting thofe offers, he fell immediately into a violent defpair.

Char. I did not hear of its violence.

' *Soph.* So violent, that he has never fince dared to
' open his lips to me about it; but to revenge the fecret
' pains I gave him, has made his public addreffes to you.

' *Char.* Indeed, fifter, you furprife me: and 'tis hard
' to fay, that men impofe more upon us, than we upon
' ourfelves.

' *Soph.*

' *Soph.* Therefore by what I have told you, you may
' now be convinced he is false to you.

' *Char.* But is there a necessity, my dear Sophronia,
' that I must rather believe you than him ? Ha, ha,
' ha !'

Soph. How, Madam ! Have you the confidence to
question my veracity, by supposing me capable of an endeavour to deceive you ?

Char. No hard words, dear sister : I only suppose you
as capable of deceiving yourself, as I am.

Soph. Oh, mighty probable, indeed ! You are a person
of infinite penetration ! Your studies have opened to you
the utmost recesses of human nature ; but let me tell
you, sister, that vanity is the only fruit of toilette lucu-
brations. I deceive myself : ha, ha, ha !

Char. One of us certainly does ! Ha, ha !

Soph. There I agree with you. Ha, ha !

Char. Till I am better convinced then on which side
the vanity lies, give me leave to laugh in my turn, dear
sister.

Soph. Oh, by all means, sweet Madam ! Ha, ha !

Both. Ha, ha, ha !

Char. Oh, here's mamma ; she perhaps may decide
the question.   Ha, ha !

Enter Lady Wrangle.

L. Wrang. So, Mrs. Charlotte ! what wonderful nothing, pray, may be the subject of this mighty merri-
ment ?

Soph. Nothing indeed, Madam ; or, what's next to
nothing ; a man, it seems.   Ha, ha !

L. Wrang. Charlotte, wilt thou never have any thing
else in thy head ?

Char. I was in hopes, nothing, that was in my sister's
head, would be a crime in mine, Madam,

L. Wrang. Your sister's ! What ? How ? Who is it
you are laughing at ?

Char. Only at one another, Madam ; but, perhaps,
your ladyship may laugh at us both : for, it seems, my
sister and I both insist, that Mr. Frankly is positively in
love but with one of us.

L. Wrang. Who, child ?

Soph. Mr. Frankly, Madam.

L. Wrang.

L. Wrang. Mr. Frankly in love with one of you!

Soph. Ay, Madam; but it seems we both take him to ourselves.

L. Wrang. Then Charlotte was in the right in one point.

Soph. In what, dear Madam?

L. Wrang. Why, that for the same reason you have been laughing at one another, I must humbly beg leave to laugh at you both——Ha, ha!

Char. So, this is rare sport.   [*Aside.*

L. Wrang. But pray, ladies, how long has the chimera of this gentleman's passion for you been in either of your heads?

Soph. Nay, Madam, not that I value the conquest; but your ladyship knows he once treated with my father upon my account.

L. Wrang. I know he made that his pretence to get acquainted in the family.

Soph. Perhaps, Madam, I have more coercive reasons, but am not concerned enough at present to insist upon their validity.

L. Wrang. Sophronia, you have prudence. [*Sophronia walks by and reads.*] But what have you to urge, sweet lady? How came this gentleman into your head, pray?

Char. Really, Madam, I can't well say how he got in, but there he is, that's certain: what will be able to get him out again, heaven knows.

L. Wrang. Oh, I'll inform you then; think no more of him than he thinks of you, and I'll answer for your cure. Ha, ha, ha!

Char. I shall follow your prescription, Madam, when I am once sure how little he thinks on me.

L. Wrang. Then judge of that, when I assure you, that his heart is utterly and solely given up to me.

Soph. Well! I did not think my Lady had been capable of so much weakness.   [*Aside.*

Char. How! to you, Madam? How is that possible, unless he makes you dishonourable offers?

L. Wrang. There's no occasion to suppose that neither; there are passions you have no notion of: he knows my

vir-

virtue is impregnable : but that———preferves him mine.

Char. Nay, this does puzzle me indeed, Madam.

Soph. If you had ever read Plato, fifter, you might have known, that paffions of the greateft dignity have not their fource from veins and arteries.

L. Wrang. Sophronia, give me leave to judge of that ; perhaps I don't infift that he is utterly Platonic neither : the manfion of the foul may have its attractions too ; he is as yet but *udum & molle lutum*——— and may take what form I pleafe to give him.

Char. Well, Madam, fince I fee he is fo utterly at your ladyfhip's difpofal, and that 'tis impoffible your virtue can make any ufe of him in my vulgar way ; fhall I beg your good word to my father, only to make me miftrefs of his mortal part ?

L. Wrang. Heavens ! what will this world come to ? ‘ This creature has fcarce been two years from fchool, ‘ and yet is impatient for a hufband ?’ No, Madam, you are too young as yet ; but———*Cruda marito.* Your education is not yet finifhed ; firft cultivate your mind, ‘ correct and mortify thefe fallies of your blood ;’ learn of your fifter here, to live a bright example of your fex ; refine your foul ; give your happier hours up to fcience, arts, and letters ; enjoy the raptures of philofophy, fubdue your paffions, and renounce the fenfual commerce of mankind.

Char. Oh, dear Madam, I fhould make a piteous phi-lefopher ; indeed your ladyfhip had much better put me out to the bufinefs I am fit for : here's my fifter has learning enough o'confcience for any one family ; and, of the two, I had much rather follow your ladyfhip's example, and ufe my humble endeavours to increafe it.

L. Wrang. My example ! Do you fuppofe then, if I had been capable of grofs defires, I would have chofen your father for the gratificator of them ?

Char. Why not, Madam ; my papa's a hale man, and though he has twice your ladyfhip's age, he walks as ftraight, and leads up a country-dance as brifk as a beau at a ball.

L. Wrang. Come, none of your fenfual inferences

from

from thence; I was governed by my parents, I had other views in marrying Mr. Wrangle.

Char. Yes, a fwinging jointure. [*Afide.*

L. Wrang. When you have gone through my ftudies, Madam, philofophy will tell you, 'tis poffible a well-natured mind, though fated to a hufband, may be at once a wife and virgin.

Char. Prodigious! [*Afide.*

L. Wrang. What is't you fmile at, Madam?

Char. Nothing, Madam, only I don't underftand thefe philofophical myfteries; but if your ladyfhip will indulge me, in marrying Mr. Frankly, as for dying a maid afterwards, I'll take my chance for it.

L. Wrang. What a giddy confidence! But thou art ftrangely vain, Charlotte, to be fo importunate for a man, that, as I have told thee, has the misfortune to be paffionately in love with me.

Char. Indeed, indeed, Madam, if your ladyfhip would but give him leave to open his mind freely, he would certainly tell you another ftory.

L. Wrang. I will fend for him this minute, and convince you of your error.

Enter a Servant.

Serv. Madam, Mr. Frankly.

L. Wrang. He never came more opportunely: defire him to walk in.

Enter Mr. Frankly.

L. Wrang. Oh, Mr. Frankly, the welcomeft man alive.

Fran. Then I am the happieft, I am fure, Madam.

L. Wrang. Oh, fy! is there any one of this company could make you fo?

Fran. There's one in the company, Madam, has a great deal more in her power, than I'm afraid fhe'll part with to me.

Soph. Are you this hard-hearted lady, fifter? Does this defcription reach you, pray? [*Afide.*

Char. The power does not defcribe you, I'll anfwer for it. [*Afide.*

L. Wrang. Nay, now you grow particular——You have fomething to fay to one of thefe ladies, I'm fure.

[*To Frankly.*

Fran.

Fran. I have fomething, Madam, to fay to both of them.

Soph. Shall we let him fpeak, fifter?

Char. Freely.

L. Wrang. Which of thefe two, now, if you were free to choofe, could you really give up your heart to?

Fran. Oh, Madam! as to that, I dare only fay, as Sir John Suckling did upon the fame occafion.

Soph. Pray, what was that?

Fran. He fure is happieft that has hopes of either;
　　　　Next him is he that fees you both together.

L. Wrang. Perfectly fine—Nor is there more wit in the verfes themfelves, than in your polite application of them—Mr. Frankly, I muft beg your pardon—I know it's rude to whifper; but you have good-nature; and, to oblige a woman——

Fran. Is the bufinefs of my life, Madam—What the devil can all this mean? I have been oddly catechized here—Sure they have not all agreed to bring me to a declaration for one of them—It looks a little like it—' But ' then, how comes Charlotte into fo vain a project? Nay, ' fo hazardous! She can't but know, my holding the ' other two in play, has been the only means of my get- ' ting admittance to her—Perhaps they may have piqued " her into this experiment— not unlikely.' But I muft be cautious. 　　　　　　　　　　　　　　[*Afide.*

L. Wrang. Nay, ladies, you can't but fay I laid you fairly in his way. [*Apart to* Soph. *and* Char.] And yet you fee from how palpable a regard to me he has ingeni- oufly avoided a declaration, for either of you, at leaft.

Soph. Your ladyfhip won't be offended, if, for a mo- ment, we fhould fufpend your conclufion.

L. Wrang. Not in the leaft; if fufpenfe can make you happy, live always in it.

Char. But, pray, Madam, let him go on a little.

L. Wrang. Oh, you fhall have enough of him. Well, you are a horrid tyrant, Mr. Frankly. Don't you plain- ly fee, here are two ladies in this company, that have a mind you fhould declare in favour of one of them?

Fran. Yes, Madam; but I plainly fee, there are three ladies in the company.

L. Wrang. What then?

ıy, then, Madam, I am more. afraid of of-
third perfon, than either of the other two.
, [*To* Soph. *and* Char.] Obferve his diffidence,
knows I love refpect.
:h fubmiffion, Madam, I never was familiar

ng. Come, now, do you both afk the quef-
have done, each exclufive of herfelf.
'our ladyfhip's in the right———[*Afide.*
ıt any apology then, I am obliged to afk you,
: be my Lady or my fifter, you are really in
?
ßo, now it's plain. [*Afide.*] When either of
ıe, you'll be out of the queftion, I can affure,
ım.
ng. Ha, ha!
/ho's in the queftion now, fifter ?
f I had put myfelf in, you would not have
:, I'll anfwer for him.   [*Afide.*
'hen, I'll do you that favour, Madam.
ıo, now the other———but I am ready for

ou fee, Sir, the humour we are in : though
ıofe, if I afk you the fame queftion, 'tis from
motive ; but fince thefe ladies have obliged
—Which of them is it you fincerely are a

ßince I find your motive is only complaifance
Madam, I hope you will not think it needs an

am fatisfied—Your ladyfhip was pleafed to
efpect—I think there's refpect and demonftra-
Madam.   [*Afide to L.* Wrang.'
. I grant it ; ' but both to me, child.' But
once more for all of us—Sir, that you may
:ed to farther ambiguities, fuppofe we are all
fhould have leave to declare which of us, then,
s utterly in the difpofal of ?
ıen I muft fuppofe, Madam, that one of you
l I fhould make the other two my enemies.
g. All your friends, depend upon us.
were all the three goddeffes to Paris, Madam,

ßill

till he prefumed to be particular, and rafhly gave the apple to Venus—You know, Madam, Juno was his immortal enemy ever after.

———— ————*Manet altâ mente repôftum*
Judicium Paridis, fpretæque injuria formæ.

L. Wrang. Sir, you are excus'd; the modefty and elegance of your reply has charmed me.

Soph. Now, fifter, was this delicacy of his tafte and learning fhewn to recommend himfelf to me or you, think you?

Char. Oh, I don't difpute its recommending him to you.

Soph. He thinks it does, depend upon't.

Char. Though I can hardly think that of him, yet I can't fay, indeed, he has taken much pains to recommend himfelf to me all this while. I fee no reafon, becaufe they are to be refpected, forfooth, that I may not be pleafed in my turn too.   [*To herfelf.*

Fran. And now, ladies, give me leave to afk you a queftion.

L. Wrang. You may command us, Sir.

Fran. Then, whofe cruel propofal was it to urge me to a declaration of my heart, when you all knew there was not one of you, from the difpofition of whofe mind or circumftances, I could hope the leaft favour or mercy.

L. Wrang. Explain yourfelf.

Fran. Why, firft, Madam, as to your ladyfhip, you are honourably difpofed of; from you my utmoft vanity could no more form a hope, than could your virtue give it—And here, [*To* Soph.] if poffible, my fate were harder ftill—here I muft have to encounter rivals numberlefs and invincible.

Soph. Rivals!

Fran. Ay, Madam, is not every volume in your library a rival? Do you not pafs whole days, nay, fometimes, happier nights, with them alone? ' The living and ' the dead promifcuous in your favour?' Old, venerable fages, even in their graves, can give you raptures, from whofe divine enjoyment no mortal lover can perfuade you.

Soph. [*To* Char.] Is this to pleafe you, fifter?

Char. Truly, I think not——he has miftaken the way, at leaft.

Fran. [*Turning to* Char.] And here, Madam——
                                        L. Wrang.

L. Wrang. Hold, Sir; a truce with your negatives, left they grow too vehement in their affirmation. You have hitherto my efteem, preferve it by your difcretion, and force me not to revoke the freedom I have this day given you. Sophronia, I have carried this matter to the very utmoft limits of difcretion. I hope you and your fifter are now delivered from your error; if not, I'll inftantly withdraw, and leave you to a full conviction. [*Exit.*

Fran. I am afraid my Lady takes fomething ill of me.

Soph. Sir, what you have done was from her own defire; and fince I partly am the occafion, it is but juft I ftand engaged for your reconciliation.

Fran. Then give me leave to hope, Madam——

Soph. From what pretenfion, Sir? From any weaknefs of my behaviour? Hope! Do you confider the licentious and extenfive confequences of that odious word? Hope! You make me tremble at the thought.

Fran. Madam, I only mean——

Soph. I know your meaning, Sir: and therefore muft not hear it.

Fran. This is new with a vengeance! [*Afide.*

Soph. Sifter, ' I am forry our argument has reduced ' me to ftand fo outrageous an inftance of your conviction; ' but you may profit from the infult:' you may now learn to moderate your vanity, and to know yourfelf. Oh, 'tis a heavenly leffon!——*E cælo defcendit gnothe feauton.* [*Exit.*

Fran. What a folid happinefs is now crept into her mind through the crack of her brain?—I hope you are not going too, Madam?

Char. I don't know any bufinefs I have here.

Fran. So——'Egad, I have difobliged them all, I believe. [*Afide.*] You are not out of humour?

Char. I don't know whether I am or no.

Fran. So cold, Charlotte, after I have had my wits upon the ftretch this half hour, to oblige you?

Char. What, in blowing up other people's vanity at my expence?

Fran. Would you have had me blown up their jealoufy, at the expence of my being well with you?

Char. You, that are fo dexterous in impofing upon others, may impofe upon me too, for ought I know.

' *Fran.*

' *Fran.* Come, come, don't impofe upon yourfelf,
' Charlotte, by this groundlefs, this childifh refentment.

' *Char.* She that has no refentment at all, may be un-
' der-treated as long as fhe lives, I find.'

Fran. Pray, think a little. Is my having made them
ridiculous by your own confent, expofing you to them,
or them to you ?

Char. I don't know how the matter's contrived ; but I
certainly find myfelf uneafy, and you can't perfuade me
I am not fo.

Fran. Well, well ; fince you can't juftify your being
in an ill humour, it's a fair ftep, at leaft, to your coming
into a good one.

Char. Come, I will not be wheedled now.

Fran. Nay, but hear me.

Sophronia *enters unfeen, while* Frankly *feems to entertain*
Charlotte *apart.*

Soph. What can thefe creatures be doing alone together ? ' I thought I left my fifter in too ill a humour to
' retire with him ; but I fee thefe carnage-lovers have
' fuch a meannefs in their fouls, they'll overlook the
' groffeft ufage to accommodate their fenfual concorpora-
' tion.' 'Tis fo—her eyes have loft all refentment already.
But I muft not be feen, left they miftake my innocent cu-
riofity for jealoufy.

Char. Well, but you might have thrown in a civil thing
to me in my turn too.

Fran. Alas, poor lady ! Pray, what one civil thing did
I mean to any body but yourfelf ? Befides, was not you
one of the three goddeffes, Mifs Charlotte ? Which of
the company do you fuppofe I meant by Venus, pray ?

Char. How filly you make me ?

Fran. Nay, I was going to fay a great deal more to you,
if my Lady had not ftopped my mouth.

Soph. Is it poffible ?   [*Afide.*

Char. Why, then, I beg your pardon ; for, in fhort, I
find I have only been fool enough to be uneafy, becaufe
they had not fenfe enough to be mortified.

Fran. A pretty innocent confeffion, truly !

Soph. Have I my fenfes ?

Char. Well, but tell me, what was it you had a mind
to fay to me ?

Fran.

Fran. Nothing to what I now could fay——Oh, Charlotte, my heart grows full of you; the leaft look of kindnefs foftens me to folly !—Indeed I love you.

Soph. Soh——

Char. And for what, after all ? [*Smiling.*

Fran. For that, and for a thoufand charms befide. [*Preffing her hand.*] There's fomething in your looks fo foft, fo gentle, fo refign'd, and plaintive ; I loved before I knew it, and only thought I gave the pity that I wanted.

Char. What tranfport's in the paffion, when the tendernefs is mutual !

Soph. Oh, the enormous creature! but I'll begone, left her intoxication fhould know no bounds—No, on fecond thoughts, I'll ftay ; ' this odious object may be ufeful; ' vipers, if rightly taken, are prefervatives : and as the ' Spartans taught their children to abhor intemperance, ' by fhewing them their flaves expofed, and fenfelefs in ' their wine ; fo I, in contemplation of this folly, may ' be fortified againft it.' Oh, the abandoned wantons !— ' What a riotous diforder now muft run through every ' vein of her whole fyftem ? How can they thus deface ' the dignity of human being ?'—[*During this* Fr. *and* Char. *feem in an amorous difpute, till he kiffes her.*]—A kifs ! nay, then, 'tis infupportable. [*She goes to them.*] Sifter, I am amazed you can ftand trifling here, when my father is come home, and you know he wants you.

Char. She has certainly feen us. [*Afide to* Fran.

Fran. No matter; feem eafy, and take no notice. [*Apart to* Char.

Soph. Shall I tell him you will not come, Madam ?

Char. Well, do not be in a paffion, dear fifter.

Fran. Oh, fie! why fhould you think fo ? But is Sir Gilbert come in, Madam ? I have a little bufinefs with him. If you pleafe, Madam, I'll wait upon you to him.

Char. With all my heart.

' *Fran. Amante fpofo,* &c. [*finging.*'
[*Exeunt* Fran. *and* Char.

Soph. What means this turbulence of thought ? ' Why ' am I thus difordered !' It cannot, nay, I will not have it jealoufy—No, if I were capable of folly, Granger might miflead me ; yet ftill I am difturbed—' Yes, 'tis

' plain, I am incenfed, provoked at him ;' but can I not
affign the caufe?—Oh, I have found it !—Having firft
offered up his heart to me, his giving it to another, without
my leave, is an infult on my merit, and worthy my refentment—that's all—How, then, fhall I punifh him? By
fecuring her to his rival. Witling fhall have her; I'll
work it by my Lady; fhe feems his friend—' Yes, yes,
' that will entirely eafe my heart. How I rejoice to find
' 'tis only decent pride that has difturbed me. Yes, I'll
' certainly refent it, to their mutual difappointment.'
Thus both fhall fuffer, doom'd to different fates:
His be defpair; be hers, the man fhe hates.

[*Exit.*

END of the SECOND ACT.

ACT III.

Lady Wrangle, *and* Sophronia.

LADY WRANGLE.

IMPOSSIBLE! You amaze me! Kifs her, fay you?
What, as a lover, amoroufly, voluptuoufly?

Soph. Infamoufly, with all the glowing fervour of a li-
bertine.

L. Wrang. Then I am deceived indeed. ' I thought
' that virtue, letters, and philofophy, had only charms for
' him : I have known his foul all rapture in their praifes;
' nay, and believed myfelf the fecret object of them all.
' But is he vulgar, brutal, then, at laft? No Punic faith
' fo falfe. 'Tis well; he has deceived me, and I hate
' him. Oh, that forward creature !

' *Soph.* She warms as I could wifh. [*Afide.*

' *L. Wrang.*' But, tell me, dear Sophronia, how did
that naughty girl behave to him? Was the fhame chiefly
his? Did fhe refift, or——' how was this odious kifs ob-
' tained? Were his perfuafions melting, or her allure-
' ments artful? Was he enfnared, or did his wiles feduce
' her?' Oh, tell me all his bafenefs! I burn to know,
yet wifh to be deceived.

Soph. —*Speratque miferrima falli*—Directly jealous of
him; but I'll make my ufes of it. [*Afide.*] Nay, Madam,

I muft

I muſt own the guilty part was chiefly hers. Had you but ſeen the warm advances that ſhe made him, ' the ' looks, the ſmiles, the toying glances; Oh, ſuch wanton ' blandiſhments to allure him!' you would think his crime, compared to hers, but frailty.

L. Wrang. Oh, the little ſorcereſs! But I ſhall ſtop her in her looſe career: I'll have her know, forward as ſhe is, her inclinations ſhall wait upon my choice; and ſince ſhe will run riot, I'll have her clogged immediately. I'll marry her, Sophronia; but. where I think fit. No, Mr. Witling is her man, or ſhe's a maid for ever.

Soph. That, Madam, I doubt, ſhe will never be brought to; ſhe mortally hates him.

L. Wrang. So much the better; I do not deſign him, therefore, as her happineſs, but her puniſhment.

Soph. This is fortunate; ſhe even prevents my purpoſe.　　　　　　　　　　　　　　　　　[*Aſide.*

L. Wrang. Oh, that a man of his ſublime faculties could fall from ſuch a height! Was ever any thing ſo mean, Sophronia?

Soph. I am ſurprized indeed. My ſiſter, too, is ſo illiterate, Madam.

L. Wrong. To contaminate his intellects with ſuch a chit of an animal; *O tempora!*

Soph. *O mores!* 'Tis a degenerate age, indeed, Madam.

' *L. Wrang.* Nothing but noiſe and ignorance; girls ' and vanity have their attractions now.

' *Soph.* Oh, there's no living, Madam, while coquettes ' are ſo openly tolerated among a civilized people!

' *L. Wrang.* I proteſt, they are ſo inſolently inſidious, ' they are become mere nuiſances to all innocent ſociety.

' *Soph.* I am amazed the government ſhould not ſet ' the idle creatures to work.

' *L. Wrang.* The wiſdom of our anceſtors reſtrained. ' ſuch horrid licences; and, you ſee, the laws they made, ' deſcribed them all by the modeſt term of ſpinſters only. But I'll take care of her, 'at leaſt; and ſince ſhe is be- ' come a public miſchief, to humble her will be a public ' good.' I'll ſend to Mr. Witling this moment, and invite him to dine here. I deſire you will be in the way, child, and aſſiſt me in bringing this matter to a ſpeedy concluſion.　　　　　　　　　　　　　　　　　[*Exit.*

　　　　　　　　　　　　　　　　　Soph.

Soph. Yes, I shall assist you, Madam; though not to gratify your resentments, but my own. Poor lady! is this then all the fruit of your philosophy? ' Is this her ' conduct of the passions, not to endure another should ' possess what she pretends to scorn? Are these her self- ' denials? Where, where was her self-examination all this ' while? The least inquiry there had shewn these passions ' as they are: then had she seen, that all this anger at ' my sister was but envy: those reproaches on her lo- ' ver, jealousy; even that jealousy, the child of vanity, ' and her avowed resentment, malice!' Good Heaven! Can she be this creature, and know it not?——And yet 'tis so—so partial's Nature to herself,

' That charity begins, where knowledge shou'd,
' And all our wisdom's counsell'd by the blood:'
The faults of others we with ease discern,
But our own frailties are the last we learn.

   [*Going off she meets* Frankly *and* Charlotte? Ha!. perpetually together!

Char. In contemplation, sister? I am afraid we disturb you: come, Mr. Frankly, we'll go into the next room.

Soph. No, Madam, if you have any secrets, I'll retire.

Char. Nay, we have none now, sister, but what I dare swear you are certainly let into: ha, ha, ha!

Fran. So she must have a gentle insult, I find; but it will be prudent in me to keep the peace.   [*Aside.*

Soph. These taunts are insupportable! but to confess the smart, were adding to her triumph.   [*Aside.*

Char. Why so grave, Sophronia?

Soph. Why that question, Madam? Do you often see me otherwise?

Char. No; but I thought, upon your supposing we had secrets, you drew up a little.

Soph. 'Tis possible, I might not be in a laughing humour, without thinking any of your secrets important.

Fran. People, Madam, that think much, always wear a serious aspect.   [*To* Char.

Soph. As the contrary, sister, may be a reason for your continual mirth.

Char. Well, well; so I am but happy, sister, I am content you should be wise as long as you live.

           Soph.

Soph. You have one fign of wifdom, I fee : a little thing contents you—There's no bearing her. [*Ex.* Soph.

Char. She's in a high miff.

Fran. I am afraid there is no good towards us : I obferved my lady, as fhe paffed too, had much the fame cloud upon her brow.

Char. Then fhe has certainly told her how fhe caught us fooling together.

Fran. No doubt on't; therefore we muft expect all the mifchief that either of them can do us.

Char. My fifter can't do us much, at leaft.

Fran. She can blow up my lady ; and, you know, my lady governs your father.

Char. She does a little overbear him indeed ; not but he will make his party good with her upon occafion : I have known it come to a drawn battle between them, efpecially when he has any body to ftand by him. A fad life though, Mr. Frankly, when conjugal engagements are only battles ; does not their example frightens you ?

Fran. I can fee no hazard, in taking my chance with you, Madam.

Sophronia *returns, and flops fhort, feeing* Frankly *taking* Charlotte's *hand.*

Soph. So ! clofing again the minute they are alone ; but I fhall make bold with them. [*Goes forward.* Pray, fifter, what did you do with that book of mine you took up this morning ?

Char. What book ?

Soph. The Confucius, you know, in my chamber.

Char. Oh, I did not mind it ; I left it upon the green table.

Soph. Very well——that's all——I beg your pardon. What a melancholy fight fhe is !.

[*Exit, and drops her handkerchief.*

Fran. This book was only a pretence to break in upon us.

Char. Plainly——fhe haunts us like the ghoft in Hamlet. But pray, what talk had you with my father juft now ?

Fran. A great deal ; we are upon very good terms there, I can tell you : but his confcience, it feems, is under the moft ridiculous dilemma, fure, that ever was.

Char. What do you mean?

Fran. If you will have patience to hear it, I'll tell you.

Char. I fhall have no patience till I do hear it.

Fran. You muft know then, fome time ago, ' Sir Gil-
' bert happened in a mixed company in Change-Alley,
' to join in a laugh at Mr.' Witling, ' for his folly (as it
' was then thought) in giving out premiums for the re-
' fufal of South-Sea ftock at an extravagant price : the
' beau being piqued to an intemperance, to fee his bar-
' gains a jeft, offered, in heat of blood, to back his judg-
' ment with more money, for a harder bargain, and ten
' times as chimerical.

' *Char.* Ay, now let's hear.

' *Fran.* Thus it was : he' told an hundred guineas into your father's hand; in confideration of which, (if
Witling could prove himfelf worth fifty thoufand pounds
within the year, and the South-Sea ftock fhould in that
time mount to a thoufand per cent. why then, and on
thofe conditions only) your father was to give him the
refufal of you, or your fifter, in marriage. ' This whim-
' fical offer turned the laugh of the company to the
' beau's fide, at which Sir Gilbert, impatient of his
' triumph, and not being in the leaft apprehenfive
' either of the ftocks rifing to that price, or that this
' rattle-headed fellow could poffibly make fuch a for-
' tune in that time, fairly took the money, and figned
' the contract.' Now the ftock, it feems, is come up to
his price, and the fpark has actually proved himfelf worth
near double the fum he conditioned for.

Char. For heaven's fake! am I to take all this feri-
oufly?

Fran. Upon my life 'tis true : but don't miftake the
matter; Sir Gilbert has left his daughter's inclinations
free : there is no force to be put upon them in the bargain.

' *Char.* Oh, then I can take my breath again.

' *Fran.* No, no; you are fafe as to that point : you
' may do as you pleafe; he has only tied up his own
' confent. But Witling having this call upon it, Sir
' Gilbert is incapable, as he fays, of giving it, at pre-
' fent, to me.

' *Char.* Well; but in the mean time, suppose he
' should give it to you; what's the penalty'?

' *Fran.* That's true; I had like to have forgot it:
' the penalty is this; if Sir Gilbert refuses his consent,
' then he is to give Witling an alternative of the three
' thousand pounds stock only, at two hundred. So low
' it seems was the price when this bargain was made.

' *Char.* A pinching article: I am afraid my good fa-
' ther has not distaste enough for a coxcomb, to part
' with his stock, and not toss him a daughter in the
' bargain.

' *Fran.* Ay, but consider; Sir Gilbert is not to part
' with his stock neither, if you refuse to marry the gen-
' tleman.'

Char. Why then the fool has given his money for
nothing; at least I am sure he has, if he makes his call
upon me.

' *Fran.* Ay, but here's the misfortune; the fool has
' been wise enough to do that already: Sir Gilbert tells
' me, he has insisted upon you; and you may be sure
' my lady, and your sister, will do all in their power to
' hold your father to his bargain: so that, while the
' contract's valid, it will not be even in your power,
' Charlotte, to complete my happiness this half year.

' *Char.* It gives me at least occasion to shew you a new
' proof of my inclination; for I confess, I shall be as
' uneasy as you, 'till, one way or other, this ridiculous
' bargain is out of that coxcomb's hands again.'

Fran. Oh, Charlotte! lay your hand upon my heart,
and feel how sensibly it thanks you.

Char. Foolish!

Sophronia *enters, as looking for her handkerchief, and ob-*
serves them.

Soph. Monstrous! actually embracing him! What
have her transports made her blind too? Sure she might
see me.

Char. Be but ruled, and I'll engage to manage it.

' *Fran.* I have a lucky thought, that certainly——'

Char. Peace! break thee off! Lo! where it comes
again.

Fran. Speak to it, Horatio——   [*Seeing* Soph.

Char. Do you want any thing, sister?

                                        Soph.

Soph. Ay! did not I drop an handkerchief here?

Char. I did not fee any——Oh, here——I believe this is it. [*Gives it her.*

[*They all ftand gravely mute for fome time, at laft; Charlotte, as uneafy at her company, fpeaks.*

Char. Do you want any thing elfe, fifter?

Soph. [*Turning fhort upon her.*]——Yes, Madam—— Patience——to fupport me under your injurious affurance.

Char. Keep your temper, fifter, left I fhould fufpect your philofophy to be only an affectation of knowledge you never could arrive at.

Soph. There are fome furprifes, Madam, too ftrong for all the guards of human conftancy.

Char. Yet I have heard you fay, Madam, 'tis a narrownefs of mind to be furprifed at any thing.

Soph. To be amazed at the actions of the unjuft, and the abandoned, is a weaknefs that often arifes from innocence and virtue: you muft therefore pardon me, if I am aftonifhed at your behaviour.

' *Fran.* So! I fuppofe I fhall have my fhare prefently.' [*Afide.*

Char. My behaviour, Madam, is not to be afperfed by outrage; and if I am not aftonifhed at yours, 'tis becaufe the folly of it ought to move no paffion but laughter.

Soph. This to me! to me, Mrs. Charlotte?

Char. Ay, ay! to you, Mrs. Sophronia.

Fran. I beg your pardon, ladies, I fee you have private bufinefs. [*Going.*

Soph. No, Sir,——hold——you are at leaft an accomplice, if not the principal, in the injury I complain of.

Fran. You do me a great deal of honour, Madam, in fuppofing any thing in my power could difturb you; but pray, Madam, wherein have I been fo unhappy as to injure you?

' *Soph.* In the tendereft part; my fame, my fenfe,
' my merit, and (as the world efteems it) in my fex's
' glory.

' *Fran.* Accumulated wrongs, indeed! But really,
' Madam,

' Madam, I am yet in the dark; I muſt beg you to ex-
' plain a little farther.'

Soph. Then plainly thus, Sir: you have robbed me
of my right; the vows of love you once preferred to
' me, are by the laws of honour, without my conſent,
irrevocable: but, like a vile apoſtate, you have ſince
preſumed to throw your ſcornful malice on my attractions, by baſely kneeling to another.

Char. Oh, the painful conflicts of prudery ! {*Aſide.*

Fran. ' This is hard indeed, Madam, that the loſs of
' what you never thought worth your acceptance, ſhould
' be worth your reſentment.' If a beggar ſhould aſk you
charity, would you call it an injury, if, upon refuſing
it, the wretch ſhould beg of the next paſſenger ?

Char. Well ; is not that prettily ſaid now, ſiſter ?

Soph. The caſe is different——You owe me tribute
as your rightful conqueror ; and though I have declined
the taſteleſs triumph of your homage, that's no remit-
tance of the duty : nor can you pay it to the uſurper of
my right, without rebellious perjury to me.

Frau. Hoyty ! toyty ! 'Egad there will be no end of
this——I muſt even talk downright to her. [*Aſide.*

Soph. Oblations vow'd to a peculiar power, are to its
peculiar altars only due ; and though the offering might
be ill-received, yet ſhould the murmuring ſuppliant dare
to invoke another's aid, his vows are then become pro-
fane and impious to the Deity.

Char. So ! ſince he would not make her a goddeſs, I
find ſhe's reſolved to make one of herſelf. [*Aſide.*

Fran. Now really, Madam, if I were to put all this
into plain Engliſh, the tranſlation would amount to no
more than this, that your offended deity is a mere dog
in a manger : what the deuce, becauſe you don't love
oats, muſt nobody elſe eat them ! Ha, ha !

Char. Ha ! ha ! ha !

Soph. Amazement ! horror ! I am ſhocked and ſhivered
to a thouſand atoms ! Oh, my violated ears !

Fran. Ay, ay ! Madam, you may give yourſelf as
many romantic airs as you pleaſe ; but, in ſhort, I can
play the civil hypocrite no longer.

Soph. Ye powers above, he triumphs in brutality !

Fran. That is, Madam, becauſe you will always take
civility,

civility for adoration. But however, to clear up this
whole matter; if, for once, you can reduce yourself from
a deity to what nature has made you, a woman of sense,
I'll beg pardon for my brutality, and speak to you like a
gentleman.

Soph. You may suppose me then to have the sense you
speak of.

Fran. Why then I own, Madam, when first I came
from travel, my good father, on whom I then depended,
recommended me to an alliance in this family: I thought
myself honoured in his commands; ' and being equally
' a stranger to you and your sister, I judged, as being the
' elder, you had a natural right to the preference of my
' addresses:' I saw you, saw your person lovely, adorned
with all those charms that usually inspire the lover's
tongue to bend the ear of beauty———

Char. How she drops her eyes at it !   [*Aside.*

Fran. But on a nearer converse, I found you scarce a
mortal in your sentiments; ' so utter a disdain of love
' had you imbibed from your romantic education: no won-
' der I succeeded not: I shall not reproach you with my
' peculiar treatment: you pleased yourself, and I re-
' treated.' On this I thought my heart at liberty to try
its better fortune here. Here I am fix'd, and justify my
love; where then is the injury to you, in laying at your
sister's feet a heart, which your disdain rejected!

Soph. 'Tis true, while offered with impure desires :
while sensually, and as a woman only, you pursued me :
but had you greatly sought the marriage of the mind,
the social raptures of the soul; I might perhaps have
cherished an intellectual union.

Fran. Ah ! but dear, dear Madam, those raptures in
the air would not do my business; I want an heir to my
family, and in plain terms my case requires one that will
give a little bodily help to it.

' *Soph.* Nay then again, I must disclaim you; a heart so
tainted would but sully the receiver : the shrine's disho-
noured by a polluted sacrifice.

Char. So ! she's at her old flights again.   [*Aside.*

Soph. Thus then I fly for ever from your hopes———

                                             Thus

Thus Daphne triumph'd o'er, Apollo's flame,
And to his heav'n prefer'd a virgin's name :
The vanquifh'd God purfu'd, but to defpair,
While deathlefs laurels crown'd the flying fair.

[Exit.

Fran. So! there's one plague over ; I have difcharged
my confcience upon her at leaft.

Char. Ha! ha! what a pretty way, though, my good
fifter has, of turning a flight into a triumph ! But fhe has
a great heart.

Fran. O! 'twould be hard to deny her that fatisfaction ;
' befide, the greateft heart in the world did juft the fame :
' we have known the late *grand monarque* lofe many a
' Battle ; but it was bloody hard to beat him out of a *Te*
' *Deum.*'

Char. Well, but now, how fhall we manage my father ?

Fran. Here he comes.

Enter Sir Gilbert.

Sir. Gilb. So, Mr. Frankly! you fee I give you fair
play——and, troth, I have a great refpect for you——
But——a——a bargain's a bargain ; if another man has
really paid for my confent, you muft not take it ill, if I
don't refufe him.

Fran. I can't pretend to afk it, Sir : I think it favour enough, if you don't oblige your daughter to refufe
me.

Sir Gilb. Not I, not I, man ; that's out of the queftion : fhe may pleafe herfelf, and if Witling fhould not
pleafe her ; troth ! I cannot fay it would not pleafe me
too : in fhort, if you two have wit enough to make up the
difference, and bring me off——why there's no more to
be faid——If not——accounts muft be made up——I
have taken the premium, and muft ftand to my contract :
for let me tell you, Sir, we citizens, are as tender of
our credit in Change-Alley, as you fine gentlemen are of
your honour at court.

Fran. Sir, depend upon it, your credit fhall not fuffer
by me, whatever it may by your comparifon.

Sir Gilb. Why, what ails the comparifon ? Sir, I think
he credit of the city may be compared to that of any bo-
ly of men in Europe.

Fran.

Fran. Yes, Sir; but you miſtake me: I queſtion if any bodies may be compared to that of the city.

Sir Gilb. O! your humble ſervant, Sir; I did not take you———ay, ay, you're right! you're right! Ay, ay, ay, live and learn, Mr. Frankly: you'll find 'tis not your court, but city politicians muſt do the nation's buſineſs at laſt. Why, what did your courtiers do all the laſt reigns, but borrow money to make war, and make war to make peace, and make peace to make war; and then to be bullies in one, and bubbles in t'other? A very pretty account truly; but we have made money, man: money! money! there's the health and life-blood of a government: and therefore I inſiſt upon it, that we are the wiſeſt citizens in Europe; for we have coined more caſh in an hour, than the tower of London in twenty years.

Fran. Nay, you govern the world now, its plain, Sir, and truly that makes us hope it's upon the mending hand: for ſince our men of quality are got ſo thick into Change-Alley, who knows but in time a great man's word may go as far as a tradeſman's?

Sir Gilb. Ah! a wag, a wag! In troth, Mr. Frankly, the more I know you, the more I like you: I ſee you know the world, you judge of men by their intrinſic value; and you're right! you're right! titles are empty things. A wiſe man will always be a wiſe man, whether he has any title or no.

Fran. Ay, ay, Sir, and when a fool gets one, he's only known to be a greater fool.

Sir Gilb. You're right again: beſides, Sir, ſhall any man value himſelf upon a thing that another may buy for his money as well as he? Ridiculous———a very pretty buſineſs truly, to give ten or twenty thouſand pounds, only to be called out of one's name: Ha, ha, ha!

Fran. Nay, Sir, and perhaps too, loſing the privilege of a private ſubject, that of being believed upon your honour, or truſted upon your word.

Sir Gilb. Honour's a joke! Is not every honeſt man a man of honour?

Fran. Ay, but the beſt joke is, that every man of honour is not an honeſt man, Sir.

Sir Gilb. Odſbodlikins, Mr. Frankly, you are an ingenious gentleman, and I muſt have you into my family,

though

though it coft me twenty thoufand pounds to keep that pragmatical fellow out on't.

Fran. ' If I have any pretence to your favour, Sir, I ' will take care your family fhall not fuffer by my coming ' into it : for if the worft muft happen,' 'tis but waiting till the other half year of Witling's contract is expired. I dare anfwer your daughter won't run away with him in the mean time.

Sir Gilb. Ay, but there's the queftion : is the girl ftaunch ? Are you fure now, that like a young hound, fhe may not gallop away with the rank fcent of a cox-comb, and fo fpoil your fport ?

Fran. ' I dare fay fhe will take this fear for a favour'— beft examine her yourfelf, Sir.

Sir Gilb. Come hither, Charlotte.

Char. Your pleafure, Sir ?

Sir Gilb. Are you fure you are as wife as other fine ladies of your age, that know more of mankind than their fathers, and confequently have a natural averfion to all hufbands of their choofing ? In fhort have you learnt enough of the world, to be heartily difobedient upon oc-cafion ?

Char. When you pleafe to give me the occafion, Sir, I will try what I can do.

Sir Gilb. Humh ! fhe promifes fair. [*To* Frankly *afide.*] The girl has wit——But now, child, the queftion is whether you have common fenfe or no (for they don't always go together.) Are you fmoky ? Have you all your eye-teeth yet ? Are you peery, as the cant is ? In fhort do you know what I would be at now ?

Char. Will you give me leave to guefs, Sir ?

Sir Gilb. Out with it.

Char. Why then, (I hope at leaft, Sir) you have a mind to make Witling believe, you are doing all in your power to bring his bargain to bear ; and at the fame time wifh I would do all in my power to bring it to no-thing.

Sir Gilb. [*Afide.*] It will do ! it will do ! Mr. Frankly ; tell her fhe's right ; you know it is not honeft for me to fay fo : a hum !

Char. In fhort, Sir, if you'll leave the matter to my difcretion, I'll engage to bring you off.

Sir Gilb. Bring me off, huffy ! why ; have you the

E   confi-

confidence to fuppofe I won't do the fair thing by the gentleman?

Char. I have not the confidence to fuppofe you would do a hard thing by this gentleman, indeed papa!

[*Takes* Frankly's *hand.*

Sir Gilb. ' D'ye hear! d'ye hear!' what a fenfible af-furance the flut has! Ah! it's a wheedling toad! [*Afide.*] Adod! I'll have a little more of her————but do you know, lady, that Mr. Witling has demanded my confent, and that it will coft me above twenty thoufand pounds to refufe it?

Char. Yes, Sir, I do know it; and if I were to give him my confent, I know that I fhould have much the worft bargain of the two.

Sir Gilb. Your confent! Why fure, Madam, when I fay, do fo, do you pretend to have a will of your own?

Char. Umh! a little! a fmall pulfe, you know, papa.

[*Fawning on* Sir Gilb.

Sir Gilb. Ah, the coaxing gipfey! why, you confident, abominable——Odfheart! I could kifs her————

Fran. Faith, do, Sir; that's no breach of your con-tract.

Sir Gilb. No! no! that's not fair neither; I am to be angry with her——befides I don't keep my word, if I don't fpeak a good one for him.

Char. That's not in your power, Sir; 'tis impoffible any body can give him a good word, at leaft to me.

Sir Gilb. How! how! will not a handfome young fellow, with an hundred thoufand pounds in his pocket, go down with you? Will not a full plumb melt in your mouth, miftrefs Dainty?

Char. Thank you, Sir; but I don't love trafh!

Sir Gilb. Trafh! Mr. Witling trafh!

Char. A coxcomb.

Sir Gilb. I fay he is————

Char. My averfion.

Sir Gilb. Bear witnefs, Mr. Frankly, fhe refufes him; you fee all I fay fignifies nothing: but I fay again and again, that I am refolved, Madam, you fhall mary him, and that articles fhall be drawn this very morning.

Char. But do you think you can't perfuade him to ftay a little, Sir?

Sir Gilb. Stay! yes; yes; a reafonable time, that is.
Char.

Char. You'll think it a reafonable one, I am fure, Sir,

Sir Gilb. Well ! well ! how long ?

Char. Only till I have done hating him, that's all.

Sir Gilb. Pfhah ! fiddle faddle ! Marry him firft, and you'll have time enough to hate him afterwards.

Char. Well, Sir, then I have but one favour to beg of you——

Sir Gilb. Come, what is't, what is't ?

Char. Only, Sir, that in the draught of the articles, you will be pleafed to leave a blank for the gentleman's name ; and if I don't fill it up to your mind, fay I know nothing of my own.

Sir Gilb. Fy ! fy ! you wicked thing you——Mr. Frankly, it will do ! it will do ! the girl has all her goings ! keep her right, keep her right, and tight ; and I'll warrant thee all fafe, boy.

Fran. Never fear, Sir——now there's but one difficulty behind ; were it but poffible to make my lady our friend in this matter——

Sir Gilb. Pfhaw ! waw ! never mind her ; am not I mafter of my own family ? Does fhe not know that my will's a law ? and if I once fay the word ——

Fran. That's true, Sir ; ' but you know, one would ' not make her a needlefs enemy :' fhe'll think herfelf affronted, take it as an infult to her underftanding, not to be let into the fecret at all.

Char. Indeed, Sir, I am afraid we fhall have a foul houfe, if fhe is not confulted in the bufinefs.

Sir Gilb. Nay, nay, with all my heart, but the foolifh woman alway loves to difpute about nothing ; and fuch a fpirit of contradiction runs away with her, I had as lief fit in the ftocks as talk to her ; however, for your private fatisfaction ——

Fran. Indeed, Sir, I think it will be better fo.

Sir Gilb. Well, well, then I'll tell her my refolution inftantly.

Char. Ah, poor papa ! What a wicked diftrefs have we brought him to ! Now will he rather run upon the mouth of a cannon, than let us fee he is afraid of gunpowder.

Fran. How my lady will bounce when he mentions it.

[*Afide.*

Sir Gilb. Oh, here's my Lady ; I'll fpeak to her now.

E 2   *Fran.*

Fran. If you pleafe, we'll retire, that you may have no interruption.

Sir Gilb. Do fo, you're right. [*Exeunt* Fran. *and* Char.
Enter Lady Wrangle, *driving a Maid Servant in before her.*

L. Wrang. Out of my doors, you dunce! you illiterate monfter! What! could you not read? Could not
you fpell? Where were your eyes, you brainlefs ideot?

Sir Gilb. Hey-day! hey-day! What's the matter now?

L. Wrag. Go, you eleventh plague of Egypt.

Maid. Indeed, Madam, I did not know it was of any
ufe, it was fo blotted and blurred, I took it for wafte paper.

L. Wrang. Blurred! you driveler! Was ever any
piece perfect, that had not corrections, rafures, interline-
ations, and improvements? Does not the very original
fhew, that when the mind is warmeft, it is never fatisfied
with its words?

Incipit, & dubitat ; fcribit, damnatque tabellas,

Et notat, & delet ; mutat, culpatque probatque.

Sir Gilb. Oh, Lord! Now the learned fit's upon her,
the devil won't be able to deal with her.   [*Afide.*

L. Wrang. What have you done with it, you dolt-
head? Where is it? Fetch it : let me fee it, I fay.

Sir Gilb. Pray, my Lady Wrangle, what is all this
rout about?

L. Wrang. Oh, nothing, to be fure! I am all always
unreafonable.

Sir Gilb. Why, look you now, did I fay any fuch thing?

L. Wrang. I don't care if you did.

Sir Gilb. It's very hard a man may not afk a civil queftion in his own houfe.

L. Wrang. Ay, do, fide with her, take her part; do,
do, uphold her in her impudence.

Sir Gilb. Why, my Lady, did I fay a word to her?

L. Wrang. Pray, Mr. Wrangle, give me leave to govern my own fervants. Don't you know, when I am out
of temper, I won't be talk'd to?

Sir Gilb. Very true, my Lady.

L. Wrang. Have not I plague enough here, do you
think?

Sir Gilb. Why ay, that's true too—Why, you confident jade! how dare you put my lady into fuch a violent
paffion?

Maid. Indeed, Sir, I don't know, not I. [*Whimpering.*
L. Wrang.

L. Wrang. Pray, Mr. Wrangle, meddle with your own business; the fault's to me, and sure I am old enough to correct her myself.

Sir Gilb. Why, what a dickens, may'nt I be of your mind neither ? 'Sheart! I can't be in the wrong on both sides.

L. Wrang. I don't know any business you have on either side.

Sir Gilb. Nay, if a man must not speak at all, it's another case.

L. Wrang. Lord! you are strangely teizing—well, come speak—what, what, what is't you would say now ?

Sir Gilb. Nay, nothing, not I ; I only asked what's the matter ?

L. Wrang. I can't tell you, the provocation's too great for words.

Sir Gilb. Well, well, well.

L. Wrang. What here still ? Am I to have no account of it then ? What have you done with it, you monster ?

Maid. Madam, the cook took it out of my hand, as I was coming down stairs with it ; he said he wanted it.

L. Wrang. The cook! run, fly, and bid the villain send it me this moment.   [*Exit Maid.*

Sir Gilb. Why, what the dickins! the senseless jade has not given him a Flanders' lac'd head to boil his cabbage in, has she ?

L. Wrang. Pshah ! Do you ever see me concern'd for such trifles ?

Sir Gilb. Or has she let the rascal singe his fowls with a bank bill ?

L. Wrang. If she had, do you think I would give myself such pain about either ?

Sir Gilb. Hah ! this must be some abominable thing indeed then.

L. Wrang. The loss, for ought I know, may be irreparable.

Sir Gilb. Oh ! then she has lost your diamond necklace, I suppose.

L. Wrang. Pray don't plague me ; 'tis impossible to express the wickedness of it.

Sir Gilb. What, the devil ! the cook has not got the slut with child, has he ?

         L. Wrang.

L. Wrang. Worfe! worfe a thoufand times!

Sir Gilb. Worfe! What than playing the whore, or thief? Then the jade has certainly committed murder.

L. Wrang. The moft barbarous that ever was——

Sir Gilb. Hoh! then fhe has broke pug's neck, to be fure. ·   [*Afide.*

L. Wrang. The changeling innocent has given that favage beaft, the cook, my whole new tranflation of the paffion of Byblis, for wafte paper, to be torn or tortur'd to a thoufand fordid ufes.

Sir Gilb. Nay then——

L. Wrang. And I have not another copy in the world, if it were to fave mankind from extirpation.

Sir Gilb. I'm glad on't, with all my heart; now could I laugh, if I durft, moft immoderately.   [*Afide.*

L. Wrang. Now, miftrefs, have you brought it?
                                                    [*Re-enter Maid.*

Maid. Madam, the cook fays, he has fkewer'd it on to the roaft-beef, and he can't take it off: he won't burn his meat for nobody, not he, he fays.

L. Wrang. Here! call the footman. He won't! Bid them drag the rafcal hither by the ears, or I'll have them nailed down to the dreffer for his impudence—I'll turn the villain out of my houfe this moment.
                                                    [*Exit Maid.*

Sir Gilb. Come, come, my Lady, don't be in a heat about a trifle; I am glad to find it's no worfe.

L. Wrang. Worfe! had he robb'd the houfe, and after fired it, I could fooner have forgiven him.

Sir Gilb. Hah! thank you for that, Madam; but I fhould not.

L. Wrang. You! you fhould not! What would be your injury compared with mine? What I'm concern'd for, the whole learned world, even to pofterity, may feel the lofs of.

Sir Gilb. Well, well; have a little patience; may be fhe may get it again. And now you talk of pofterity, my lady Wrangle, I have fome thoughts of marrying my daughter Charlotte; as for Sophronia, you know——

L. Wrang. I know, that one won't, and t'other fhan't marry; fhe is a pert forward thing, and has difobliged me, and therefore I'll punifh her as I think fit. I defire
                                                    you

you won't name her to me, you fee I have other things in my head—all greas'd, and burnt to aſhes, I ſuppoſe.

Sir Gilb. I had better talk to her another time, I believe.

Enter the Maid with the Cook.

L. Wrang. Oh! are you come at laſt, Sir? Pray, how durſt you ſend me ſuch an impudent anſwer?

Cook. I did not ſend an impudent anſwer, Madam; I only ſaid the meat would be ſpoil'd: but here ſhe comes, and makes a noiſe, and a rout, and a clatter about nothing at all—and ſo every impertinent jade here takes upon her—Oons! a man can't do his buſineſs in quiet for them.

L. Wrang. Hold your nonſenſical tongue, Sir, and give me the paper I ſent for.

Cook. Paper! This is what ſhe gave me.

[*Holds it on a ſkewer, all greaſy.*

L. Wrong. Oh my heavens! what a ſpectacle! not one line legible, though an empire were to purchaſe it. Look, look, look, you monſter! [*Holding him.*

Sir Gilb. So! here will be rare doings.

Cook. Oons! what a life's here about a piece of foul paper?

L. Wrang. A life, you villain! your whole life can't make amends for what you have done. I'll have you beat out of this houſe, till every bone in your body is broken for this, ſirrah.

Cook. Beat, Madam! Blood! I won't be beat. I did not come here for that: I'll be out of your houſe preſently; I'll ſee who will break my bones then; and ſo there's one of your napkins, Madam: as for your ſheet of paper, there's a half-penny for't; and now take your courſe. I know how to get my wages, I'll warrant you—There's a law for ſervants as well as other people.

[*Exit Cook.*

Sir Gilb. Go, go, mind your buſineſs, you ſilly Tom Ladle you.

L. Wrong. Ay; this is always the effect of your indulgence; no wonder I have no power over them. If you had the leaſt grain of ſpirit, you would have broke the raſcal's head for me.

Sir Gilb. Pſhah! there's no occaſion for it—let's ſee,
let's

let's fee! [*Takes up the paper.*] Come, come, this matter may be made up without bloodshed still—ay, here; umh! umh!—by the way, I believe this beef's enough, it smells bravely of the gravy.

L. Wrang. What! then I am your jest, it seems.

Sir Gilb. Pooh! pry'thee be quiet; I tell you, I am serious——ay, it's plain to be read still.   [*Reads.*

All a poor maid could do (the gods, I'm sure,
Can tell) I've suffer'd to compleat my cure—Cure!
Ah, poor soul —— got the foul disease, I suppose.

L. Wrang. Your obscene comment, Mr. Wrangle, is more provoking than the insolence of your servants: but I must tell you, Sir, I will never eat or sleep in your house more, if that rascal is not turned out of it this moment.

Maid. I hope your Ladyship is not in earnest, Madam.

L. Wrang. What do you prate, Mrs. Minx?

Maid. Indeed, Madam, if John's to be turn'd away, I shan't stay in the family: for though he is sometimes a little hasty to a body, yet I have reason to know he is an honest-hearted man in the main; and I have too much kindness for him to stay in any service, where he is to be abus'd.

L. Wrang. What, you are in love with him, Mrs. Trollop, are you?   [*Cuffs her.*

Maid. Ods my life! Madam, I won't be struck by no body: and if I do love him, what's that to any body? and I don't know why poor folks mayn't be in love as well their betters.

Sir Gilb. Come, come, hold your tongue, hussy.

Maid. Sir, I can't hold my tongue; though I can't say but your worship's a very kind master: but as for my Lady, the devil would not live with her; and so, Madam, I desire you will provide yourself.   [*Flings off.*

Sir Gilb. Odzines, Madam, at this rate I shall have neither dinner to eat, nor bed to lie on. What servants will bear this life, do you think? You have no more temper than a——Why how should a silly wench know what your impertinent poetry was good for?

L. Wrang. Impertinent! I'd have you know, Mr. Ignorant, there's not a line in the whole, that has not the true Attic salt in it.

                                        Sir

Sir Gilb. Well, and now there's English salt in it ; and I think the relish of one's as good as t'other.

L. Wrang. Mr. Wrangle, if you have no sense of the soul's diviner faculties, know, I have, and can resent these vulgar insults. You shall find, Sir, that a superior understanding has a proportion'd spirit to support its dignity. Let me have instant reparation, or, by my injured genius, I'll set you house and family in a blaze.

[*Exit L.* Wrang.

Sir Gilb. Why then blaze and burn by yourself; for I'll go out of the house. [*Going.*

Enter Frankly *and* Charlotte.

Fran. Have you seen my Lady, Sir ?

Sir Gilb. Yes, yes, I have seen her—but—I don't know——she——she——

Fran. Don't come into it, I suppose.

Sir Gilb. Umh ! no, not readily——in short, the house is all untiled.

Char. Lord, Sir ! what filthy thing's this ?

[*Seeing the Paper.*

Sir Gilb. Ay, there's the business——a brat of my Lady's brain, that has got a mischance : that's all.

Fran. Some roasted poetry, I presume.

Sir Gilb. Ay, ay ; the, the, the passion of Bibble Babble ; I don't know what she calls it : but she has been in such a fume here, that half the servants are going to leave the house about it. Charlotte, you can wheedle upon occasion ; pry'thee step into the hall, and see if you can make up this matter among them.

Char. I'll do my best, Sir. [*Exit* Char.

Fran. Poor Lady ! she is a little apt to be over-concerned for her poetry.

Sir Gilb. Concern'd ! Odsblews ! if a line on't happens to be mislaid, she's as mad as a blind mare that has lost her foal ; she'll run her head against a stone-wall to recover it. All the use I find of her learning is, that it furnishes her with more words to scold with.

Enter a Servant.

Serv. Sir, Mr. Grainger's come, and Mr. Witling.

Sir Gilb. Oh, that's well. Come, Mr. Frankly, let's all go into the dining-room together ; mayhap she may be asham'd to be in a passion before company.

Fran.

Fran. At leaſt we may keep her within bounds, Sir.

Sir Gilb. You're right ! you're right ! Ah ! its a very hard caſe ! there's no condition of life without plague and trouble——Why, moſt people think now I have fortune enough to make ten men of quality happy——

And yet you ſee how odly things are carried ;

'Tis true, I'm worth a million, but I'm married.

[*Excunt.*

A C T   IV.

Granger *and* Frankly.

FRANKLY.

IN one word, Granger, thou art a very dangerous fellow ; ' I did not believe it poſſible thy blunt humour could have concealed ſo exquiſite a flatterer :' why thou art more in my lady's favour in half an hour, than all my art could make me in half a year.

Gran. Have I not always told you, Frankly, that one civil thing from a downright dealer, goes farther than a thouſand from a man of general complaiſance ? ' How do ' you think I firſt gain'd credit with Sophronia ? Not (as ' you expected to do it) by an implicit admiration ; but ' the contrary, inſolently laughing at her pretending to ' principles, which I would not allow her capable to com- ' prehend or practiſe. Now this naturally piqued her in- ' to an impatience to mend my opinion of her ; ſo the ' more difficult I ſeemed to be convinced of her virtues, ' the more eaſy I made it to mend her opinion of me.'

Fran. And if thou haſt not done it effectually, I know nothing of the ſex : why, ſhe bluſh'd, man, like a damaſk roſe, when you firſt came into the room.

Gran. Did not I tell you too, her quarrel and ſpleen to you would be of ſervice to me ?

Fran. O ! palpably ! I was ready to burſt to ſee her bridle, and ſmile at me, upon your growing particular to her.

Gran. And what pains ſhe took, to make you obſerve, that ſhe overlooked you ? ha ! ha !

' *Fran.* Yes, I did obſerve, indeed, that the whole

' dinner-

' dinner-time fhe was never two minutes without ftealing
' a glance at you.
' *Gran.* O blefs me! I can't bear the infolence of my
' own imagination! What a dear confufion will fhe feel?
' What a vermilion fhame will fpread through all that
' lovely form——if ever her flefh and blood fhould hap-
' pen to mutiny?
' *Fran.* Which, to tell you the truth, I think it does
' already.'

Gran. But the misfortune is, I have flatter'd my lady
into fo good a humour, by engaging to make out a fair
copy of her bafted verfes there, that I doubt, fhe won't
be able to leave me alone with Sophronia.

Fran. Never fear; her malice is too bufy, in fetting
Witling againft me, to interrupt you.

Gran. There, indeed, I have fome hopes.

Fran. I believe I fhall be able to affift them, and in
part to return the favour you have done me with Sir Gilbert.

Gran. Any thing in my power you may be fure of——
but fee, he's here!

Enter Sir Gilbert.

Sir Gilb. O! your fervant, gentlemen; I thought we
had loft you.

Gran. Your pardon, Sir, we had only a word or two
in private,

Fran. We were juft coming into the company.

Sir Gilb. In troth, I can tell you, the fooner the better: for there's my lady and Charlotte are going to play
all the game upon us.

Fran. Never fear, Sir; as long as you have given me
leave to go Charlotte's halves, fhe'll make the moft of her
cards, I'll warrant you.

Sir Gilb. I don't know that, but I am fure Witling
yonder is making the moft of his time: his wit, or his
impudence have got him into fuch high favour with my
lady, that fhe is railing at you like a fury, and crying
him up for an angel: in fhort, Charlotte has difcovered
all your affair with her, and has plainly told him you are
his rival. But it feems, Sir, your pretenfions are fo
ridiculous, that they are all three cracking their fides in a
full chorus of laughing at you.

3 *Fran.*

Fran. Sir, I am obliged to you for your concern ; but in all this, Charlotte is acting no wrong part, I can assure you.

Sir Gilb. No wrong part! Odsheart ! I tell you she's coquetting to him, with every wicked limb about her — and is as full of her airs there, as a handsome widow to a young lord in the Lobby, when she has a suit depending in the House of Peers.

Fran. Better still, the more likely to carry her cause, Sir.

Sir Gilb. Carry her cause! carry her coxcomb, Sir ; for, you'll see, that will be the end on't : she'll be carry'd off herself, Sir. Why, man, he is going to beleaguer her with a whole army of fidlers yonder ; ' there ' are six coach loads of them now at the door, all stow'd ' fore and aft, with nothing but cases of instruments :' Such a concourse of cat-guts, you'd swear one of their squalling eunuchs were roasting alive here.

Fran. Believe me, Sir, there is no terror in all this preparation ; ' for since you are pleased to think Mr. ' Granger's security and mine sufficient against any da- ' mage you can suffer from your contract with Witling,' do you but stand it out stoutly with my lady, and I'll engage to dismount his musical battery with a child's whistle.

Sir Gilb. My lady ! Pshaw waw ? What dost thou talk of her, man ? Why I tell you, I'll put her into a mousehole, provided you engage to bring me off with Witling.

Gran. Your security shall be signed the minute it can be drawn, Sir.

Sir Gilb. That's enough ; ' I have ordered my lawyer ' to send his clerk with it, before he brings the deed of ' consent that I am to sign to Witling, :' but give me leave to tell you again, gentlemen, I really don't understand the girl's way of proceeding all this while.

Fran. Why, Sir——don't you know that Witling is the vainest togue upon earth.

Sir Gilb. I grant it.

' *Fran.* And consequently, that the pride of outwit- ' ting you in your daughter, gives him more pleasure than ' either her person or her portion ?

' *Sir Gilb.* Not unlikely.

' *Fran.*

' *Fran.* And can you think, that from the fame natural
' infolence, he would not rather feem to owe his triumph
' over a rival too, rather to his own merit, than any ac-
' cident of fortune ?
' *Sir Gilb.* I grant you that too.'

Fran. Why, Sir, then, if Charlotte were to defpife
him, we are fure he would then infift upon his bargain ;
but while fhe flatters him, and you and I only laugh at
him, he may be vain enough to truft his triumph to her
choice and inclination only.

Sir Gilb. O! now I begin to take you : fo that, if he
is rightly handled among us, you propofe that Charlotte
will be able to coquette him out of his contract.

Fran. Nay, it's her own project, Sir : and I cannot
really think we have an ill chance for it at worft : but we
muft leave it all to her now. In love affairs, you know,
Sir, women have generally wifer heads than we.

Sir Gilb. Troth! I don't wholly diflike it ; and if I
don't handle him roundly on my part—

Gran. Hufh ! my lady——

Fran. Anon I'll tell tell you more, Sir.

      Enter Lady Wrangle *and* Sophronia.

L.Wrang. Well, Sophronia, fince I fee this giddy girl is
neither to be formed by precept or example ; it is at leaft
fome confolation, to find her natural inconftancy fo effectually mortifies that vile apoftate, Frankly.

Soph. Yet I am amazed he fhould not be more moved at
her infidelity.

L. Wrang. You know he's vain, and thinks his merit
may fleep in full fecurity. But now ! to roufe him from
his dream—— Oh, Mr. Granger! I am forry you left
us ; I am perfectly killed with laughing ! There's Mr.
Witling has had fuch infinite humour ! He has entertain'd
as more than ten comedies.

Gran O! Pray, Madam, let us go in and participate.

L. Wrang. By no means ; he's now alone with his
miftrefs, and 'twould be barbarous to interrupt them.

Gran. His miftrefs, Madam !

L. Wrang. Ay ! with Charlotte ; and, you know,
lovers fo near their happinefs are apt to like no company
fo well as their own.

Fran.

Fran. D'ye hear, Sir ?   [*To* Sir Gilb. *apart.*
Sir Gilb. I told you how it was.   [*To* Fran. *apart.*
L. Wrang. Befide, he is to give us a little mufic ; and I think this room will be more convenient.

Gran. He is a fortunate man indeed, Madam, to be fo well with the young lady already.

L. Wrang. There's no accounting for that idle paffion in uncultivated minds : I am not furprifed at her for-wardnefs, confidering the vulgar education Mr. Wrangle has given her.

Sir Gilb. Odfheart, Madam ! don't difparage my girl : fhe has had a more ufeful education than your ladyfhip.

L. Wrang. O ! no doubt ! fhe has fhewn moft hopeful effects on it, indeed ! by hanging upon every young fel-low's neck, that does but afk her the queftion.

Fran. Whatever faults Charlotte may have, Madam, I never knew her take pleafure in expofing thofe of other people.

' *L. Wrang.* O ! cry you mercy, Sir; you have great
' reafon to defend her, I don't queftion : fhe is a faint in
' your eye, to be fure.

' *Fran.* Were fhe weak enough to imagine a fuperficial
' learning could make her one, 'tis poffible, her failings
' then, like other people's, might have been more con-
' fpicuous.'

L. Wrang. What do you mean, Sir?

Fran. I mean, Madam, that as fhe does not read Ari-otle, Plato, Plutarch, or Seneca, fhe is neither roman-tic or vain of her pedantry ; and as her learning never went higher than Bickerftaff's Tatlers, her manners are confequently natural, modeft, and agreeable.

Sir Gilb. Ah ! well faid Frankly.   [*Afide.*

L. Wrang. Since I am told you were once in love with her, I fhall fay 'no more, but leave her own immediate behaviour to confirm your good opinion of her virtues. Ha, ha !   [*Exit.*

' *Gran.* While the lovers of this age, Madam, have
' fo deprav'd a tafte, we muft not wonder, if our modern
' fine ladies are apt to run into coquettry : they are now
' forced to it in their defence; if they don't make
' advances, they ftand as lonely and ufelefs as untenan-
' ted houfes : fo that coquetry, it feems, is no more than
          — ' fetting

' fetting a bill upon their door, that lovers in diſtreſs
' may read as they paſs——Here are night's lodgings to
' be let.

' *L. Wrang.* O! they are moſt hoſpitable dames in-
' deed: after this, methinks, the more proper appella-
' tion for coquets ſhould be that of landladies.

[*A ſervant whiſpers* L. Wrang.
' I'll come and give orders myſelf. [*Exit.*

Soph. I don't know any man alive, that looks upon the
degeneracy of mankind with ſo diſcerning an eye as Mr.
Granger; but I am afraid it will therefore draw him into
my misfortune, of being as odious to the illiterate of his
ſex, as I am to thoſe of mine.

Gran. If that were as juſt a reaſon, Madam, for your
having a favourable opinion of me, as it is for my perfect
admiration of you, we ſhould each of us have ſtill as many friends as any wiſe man or woman ought to deſire.

Fran. Do you mind that, Sir? [*Apart.*

Sir Gilb. A ſly rogue! he knows how to tickle her up,
I ſee. [*Apart.*

Soph. And yet the rude world will ſay, perhaps, that
our mutual enmity to them has reduced us to a friendſhip
for one another.

Gran. That's a reproach can never reach you, Madam:
ſo much beauty cannot but have its choice of friends and
admirers: a form ſo bright and perfect, like a comet in
the hemiſphere, where'er it comes, muſt ſet mankind a
gazing.

Soph. Fye! Mr. Granger!

Sir Gilb. What, a dickens! will ſhe ſwallow that bla-
zing ſtar now? [*Apart.*

Fran. Ay, as he has dreſs'd it, and drink after it too,
Sir. [*Apart.*

Soph. I mind not multitudes.

Gran. Pardon me, I know you have a ſoul above them;
and I really think it the misfortune of your perſon, to
have been ſo exquiſitely fair, that where your virtue would
preſerve, your eyes deſtroy; they give involuntary love;
where'er you paſs, in ſpite of all your innocence, they
wound *Juvenumque prodis publica cura.*

Soph. Alas! my eyes are turn'd upon myſelf: ' and ſo
' little do I mind the follies of other people, that I ſome-
F 2 times

' times find myfelf alone in the midft of a public circle.

' *Gran.* I cannot wonder at that, Madam, fince our beft
' affemblies are generally made up of illiterate beings, that
' when they are alone, find themfelves in the worft com-
' pany, and fo are reduced to come abroad, though mere-
' ly to meet, and hate one another.'

Soph. What charms, then, can you fuppofe I could
have for a world, that has fo few for me ? Befide, at moft,
the men of modern gallantry gaze upon a woman of real
virtue, only as atheifts look into a fine church, from curio-
fity, not devotion : ' they may admire its ornaments and
' architecture ; but have neither grace nor faith for far-
' ther adoration.'

Gran. All men are not infidels ; of me, at leaft, you
have a convert : and tho' the fenfual practice of the
world had made me long defpair of fuch perfection in a
mortal mold ; yet when the rays of truth celeftial broke
in upon my fenfe, my confcious heart at once confefs'd
the deity ; I proftrate fell a profelyte to virtue ; and
now its chafte defires enlarge my foul, and raife me to fe-
raphic joy.

Soph. Harmonious founds, celeftial tranfports ! [*Afide.*

Sir Gilb. Oh, dear ! Oh, dear ! was ever fuch a wicked
thief ? Odfheart, he'll make her go to prayers with him,
prefently ! [*Afide.*

Soph. No more ; we are obferved. Thefe heaven-born
emanations of the foul defire not vulgar ears. Some fitter
time may offer—till when———

Gran. Till then, be hufh'd our joys.

[*Gran. leaves her, and joins the men, while* Soph. *walks
apart, mufing.*

Soph. Our joys indeed ! Such was, in Paradife, our firft
parents joy, before they fell from innocence to fhame.

Fran. [*To* Gran.] Why did you not go on with her ?
We thought you were in a fine way. Sir Gilbert and I
were juft going to fteal off.

Gran. Soft and fair, Sir. A lady of her delicacy muft
be carried, like a taper new-lighted, gently forward ; if
you hurry her, out fhe goes.

Sir Gilb. You're right, you're right. Now you fhall
fee me manage her a litle : I'll fpeak a good word for you
—a-hum—

Gran.

Gran. Hufh ! not for the world, Sir——Death, you'll fpoil all ! Don't you fee fhe is in contemplation ?

Sir Gilb. What if fhe be, man ? We muſt not humour her till fhe is ſtark mad, neither. Sophronia, how doſt thou do, child ?

Soph. [*Repeating.*]———— ——The earth
Gave fign of gratulation, and each hill :
Joyous the birds ; freſh gales and gentle airs
Whiſper'd it to the woods, and from their wings
Flung rofe, flung odours, from the juicy fhrub
Diſporting————

Sir Gilb. Very pretty, I proteſt ; very pretty. Thefe amorous fcraps of fancy in thy head, make me hope that love is not far from thy heart, Sophy.

Soph. Love, Sir, was ever in my heart ; but fuch a love, as the blind Homer of this Britiſh iſle, in rhymeleſs harmony, fublimely fings————

Sir Gilb. Well, and, pr'ythee, what does he fay of it ?

Soph. ———- ———— Love refines
The thought, and heart enlarges ; has his feat
In reafon, and is judicious, is the fcale,
By which to heavenly love thou mayſt afcend.

Sir Gilb. Very good again ; and troth, I'm glad to hear thou art fo heartily reconciled to it.

Soph. Eafier than air with air, if fpirits embrace,
Total they mix, union of pure with pure
Defiring————

Sir Gilb. Ah ! there, I doubt, we are a little crazy.
[*Afide.*

Soph. This iron age, fo fraudulent and bold,
Touch'd with this love, would be an age of gold.

Sir Gilb. Oh, lud ! Oh, lud ! this will never do. [*Afide.*

Gran. So, fhe has given the old gentleman his belly-full, I fee. Well, Sir, how do you find her ?

Sir Gilb. Ah, poor foul, piteous bad ! all upon the tantivy again ! You muſt e'en undertake her yourſelf ; for I can do no good upon her. But here comes love of another kind.

Enter Charlotte, Witling, *and Lady* Wrangle.

Char. Oh, fiſter ! here's Mr. Witling has writ the prettieſt cantata, fure, that ever made mufic enchanting.

Soph. I am glad, fifter, you are reconciled to any of his performances.

Wit. Oh, fie! Madam, fhe only rallies——A mere trifle.

Fran. That I dare fwear it is.

Wit. Ha, ha! no doubt on't; if you could like it, it muft be an extraordinary piece, indeed, Tom. You fee, my little rogue, we have crabbed him already.

                        [*Afide, to* Char.

L. Wrang. Mr. Frankly is a mere modern critic, that makes perfonal inclination the rule of his judgment; but to condemn what one never faw, is making fhort work, indeed.

Fran. With fubmiffion, Madam, I can fee no great rafhnefs in prefuming that a magpye can't fing like a nightingale.

Wit. No, nor an owl look like a peacock, neither. Ha, ha!

L. Wrang. and Char. Ha, ha, ha!

L. Wrang. Perfectly pleafant.

Char. Oh, wit to an infinity!

Fran. Much good may do you with your Canary-bird, Madam.   [*To* Char.

Char. Oh, Sir, I am forry you are exhaufted! but when wit is upon the lee, no wonder it runs into rudenefs.

' *Fran.* I don't wonder at my not hitting your tafte, ' Madam, when fuch ftuff as this can go down with you.

' *Wit.* My ftuff, dear Tom, was compofed purely for ' the entertainment of this lady; and fince fhe likes it, I ' will allow, that you, of all mankind, have moft reafon ' to find fault with it. Ha, ha!

' *Char.* Nay, if he fhould like it, even I will then give ' it up, to the world as good for nothing.

' *Fran.* Then it's in danger, I can tell you, Madam; ' for I fhall certainly like it; becaufe I am fure it will ' be good for nothing.

' *Char.* A pleafant paradox.

' *Fran.* None at all, Madam; for fince I find your ' heart is, like ftock, to be transferred upon a bargain, it ' will be fome pleafure, at leaft, to fee the groffnefs of ' your choice revenge me on your infidelity.

                                     ' *Wit.*

' *Wit.* Poor Tom ! What, are the grapes four, my
' dear ? Ha, ha, ha !

' *Char.* Pſhah ! never mind him. The cantata, dear
Mr. Witling, the cantata.

L. Wran. Oh, by all means ! ' Pray oblige us, Sir.

' *Wit.* Immediately, Madam ; but all things in order.
' Firſt give me leave to regale the good company with a
' ſmall craſh of inſtrumental.

' *L. Wrang.* As you pleaſe, Sir.

' *Wit.* Hey, Signor Carbonelli ! *Vi pace d'intrare !*

[*The muſic enter.*

' *L. Wrang.* Mr. Granger, won't you pleaſe to ſit ?

' *Sir Gilb.* Ay, ay, come, gentlemen ; but, in earneſt,
' does this puppy really pretend to ſing ?

' *Fran.* Much as he pretends to wit, Sir ; he can
' make a noiſe, at leaſt.

' *Sir Gilb.* But the whelp has no voice.

' *Fran.* Oh, Sir, that's out of faſhion ! Your beſt ma-
' ſters ſeldom have any.

' *Sir Gilb.* Then I would not give a fig for their mu-
' ſic, Sir ; I would as lief ſee a cripple dance. But let's
' hear what the fiddles can do. [*They play a ſonata.*]
' Well, and what, we are to ſuppoſe this is very fine,
' now, ha ?

Fran. No doubt on't, Sir ; at leaſt it will not be ſafe
' to ſay the contrary.

' *Sir Gilb.* Well, well, for a quiet life, then, very fine
' let it be ; but I wiſh I could hear a Lancaſhire horn-
' pipe for all that.'

L. Wrang. Come, dear Sir, no more apologies.

[*To* Witling.

Gran. See, Sir, Mr. Witling is going to entertain us.

Sir Gilb. Ay, that muſt be rare ſtuff indeed.

' *Wit.* Upon my life, Madam, I have no more voice
' than a kettle-drum ; beſide, this is for a treble, and out
' of my compaſs.

' *Char.* Oh, no matter ? feign it, dear Mr. Witling.

' *Wit.* I would fain oblige you, Madam ; but yet, me-
' thinks, nothing done to pleaſe yeu ſhould be feign'd,
' neither, Madam.

' *Fran.* Ha ! He would fain be witty, I ſee ; but don't
' trouble yourſelf, Madam ; he has as much min'l to ſing

' as

‘ as you have to hear him: tho', Heaven knows, his voice
‘ is like his modefty, utterly forced ; nature has nothing
‘ to do with either of them.

‘ *Wit.* Whatever my modefty is, dear Tom, thy unea-
‘ finefs I am fure is natural ; that comes from thy heart,
‘ I dare anfwer for it. Ha, ha, ha !

‘ *Fran.* Oh, thou happy rogue !.’

Wit. But, Madam, if I fing, you fhall promife me to
dance, then.

Char. Oh, any compofition ! I'll do it with all my
heart.

L. Wrang. But the words ‘ firft, dear Sir, read them
‘ out.’

Wit. Well, ladies, fince you will have it——

Sir Gilb. He is a curfed while about it, methinks——

Wit. You muft know, then, this cantata is of a different
fpecies from the paffion generally expreffed in our modern
operas ; for there you fee your lover ufually approaches
the fair lady with fighs, tears, torments, and dying. Now,
here I fhew you the way of making love like a pretty fellow ; that is, like a man of fenfe, all life, and gaiety——
As for example——

Char. Pray, mind.

Wit. [*Reading.*]

> Thus to a penfive fwain,
> Who long had lov'd in vain,
> Thyrfis, the fecret arts
>   Of gaining hearts
>   From cold difdain,
> To his defpairing friend imparts.

So far recitative—Now for the air—A hum, hum !

‘ *Soph.* Don't you think, Mr. Granger, that the double
‘ dative cafes of “ to a penfive fwain, to his defpairing
‘ friend,” almoft reduce this to nonfenfe ?

‘ *Gran.* Juftly obferved, Madam ; but, you know,
‘ nonfenfe and harmony are reconciled of late.’

Wit.   Would you woo her
>   With fuccefs ?
>   Up to her,
>   Purfue her
> With life and addrefs.

If gay,
Shew her play;
If colder,
Be bolder:

Now feize her,
And teize her,
And kifs her,
And pleafe her;
Till ripe for the joy,
You warm her,
Alarm her,
Difarm her,
You charm her,
I warrant thee, boy.

Part II.

But to pine and languifh,
 Or figh your anguifh
 To the air,
 Is fruitlefs pain,
 Endur'd in vain:
Silent woes, and looks of care,
Will never, never win the fair.

End with the firft ftrain.

Ah, you little rogue!   [*To* Charlotte.
 L. Wrang. Infinitely pretty! ' Nothing, fure, was ever
' fo mufical.
 ' *Char.* Sing it, fing, it, dear Mr. Witling.   I am on
' tiptoe to hear it.
 ' *Wit.* Well, Madam, if you can bear it in a falfetto.
                                            [*He fings.*
 ' *Char.* O caro! caro!
 ' *Wit. Anima mia*——
Soph. [*To* Gran.] How happy are the felf-conceited!
' and yet, if he had not fung, now, this wretch's folly
' and ignorance had been lefs confpicuous.
 ' *Gran.* Right, Madam; but, you know, a man muft
' have variety of parts, to make an accomplifhed cox-
' comb.
                                            ' *Soph.*

' *Soph.* I fcarce think poetry is more abufed than mu-
' fic, by its vain pretenders.
' *Gran.* And yet it is hard to fay, Madam, whether
' thofe pretenders, or the falfe tafte of our modern ad-
' mirers, have more contributed to the abufe of either.'

Wit. But come, Madam, now your promife ; ' your
' airs only' [*To* Char.] can give a *bonne bouche* to our
entertainment.

Char. Well, fince I gave my word, I'll ufe no ceremony.

Soph. ' What, more folly ?' I grow tired. Shall we walk
into my library ? There we may raife our thoughts.

Gran. You charm me, Madam ; I thirft, methinks,
for a clear draught of Helicon.

Soph. Take no leave, but follow me. [*Ex.* Soph. *&* Gr.

Wit. ' *E ben fonate.*' [Charlotte *dances.*] ' *Eh ! viva !*
' *viva !*' All enchantment, Madam ! no ten thoufand
angels ever came up to it.

L. Wrang. It cannot be denied but Charlotte has an ex-
ternal genius; fhe wants no perfonal accomplifhments ; but
'tis great pity the application they have coft her, was not
laid out upon the improvement of her underftanding.

Wit. Oh, pardon me, Madam ! as long as there is a
good underftanding between her and me, what matter's
which of us has it, you know.

Sir Gilb. Ay, but there's the queftion, which of you
'tis that has it ; for if one of you has it, I am fure you
two will never come together.

Fran. Well faid ! at him, Sir. [*Afide.*

Wit. Look you, Sir Gilbert ; you may fancy your fair
daughter and I are a couple of fools, if you pleafe ; but if
one of us had not been wifer than the father, we could
never have had a right to come together, in fpite of his
teeth, that's certain. Ha, ha, ha !

L. Wrang. Pardon me, Mr. Witling, you under-rate
your merit ; for you had been fure of my confent without
your contract.

Wit. Ay, Madam, that was only a foolifh modefty that
I could not fhake off ; therefore I hope you will excufe
me, if durft not think merit alone was a fufficient bait to
bob Sir Gilbert out of his confent. Ha, ha, ha !

' *Sir Gilb.* You are a very merry grig, Sir ; but have a
care you are not bobb'd yourfelf. Stay till you win, before
you laugh ; for you are not yet married, I prefume.

Wit.

Wit. Why no, nor you have not fupped yet; yet I hold gold to filver, we both eat before we fleep.

Sir Gilb. Why! doft thou think the girl is in hafte to marry thee to night!

Wit. I don't fay that neither: but, Sir, as long as I have a fufficient depofit of the lady's inclinations, to anfwer for the reft of her premifes, you will give me leave not to be afraid of her looking out for a new chap in the mean time, Sir.

Sir Gilb. A depofit! why wouldft thou perfuade me the girl can be fool enough to like thee?

Wit. 'Egad, I don't know how it is, but fhe has wit enough, it feems, to make me think fo——but if you won't take my word, let her anfwer for herfelf.

Sir Gilb. Ay, that I would be glad to hear.

Wit. Ha, ha! 'Egad, this is a pleafant queftion indeed ——Madam, are not you willing, (as foon as the church-books can be open) to make a transfer of your whole ftock of beauty for the conjugal ufes of your humble fervant?

Char. Indeed, papa, I won't fuppofe that can be a queftion.

Wit. A hum! your humble fervant, Sir.

Char. Befide, are not you obliged to fign a further deed of confent to Mr. Witling?

Sir Gilb. Yes, child; but the fame deed referves to you a right of refufal, as well as to him.

Char. That I underftand, Sir; and there's one can witnefs for whom I have referved that right of refufal.

[*Pointing to* Fran.

Wit. Your humble fervant, again, Sir; ha, ha, ha!

L. Wrang. I am amazed, Mr. Wrangle, you could think fhe could be under the leaft difficulty in the choice.

Fran. And yet, Madam, there are very innocent ladies, that have made a difficulty of changing their inclinations in half an hour.

L. Wrang. A woman of ftrict virtue, Sir, ought to have no inclinations at all: or, if any, thofe only of being obedient to the will of her parents.

Wit. Oh, let him alone, Madam; the more he rails, the more I fhall laugh, depend upon't: the pain of a rival is the pleafanteft game in the world: his wifhing me at the devil, is juft the fame thing as if he wifhed me joy! ha, ha, ha!

Sir Gilb. Well, Sir, all I shall say, is, that if the girl has common sense, thy contract must still be good for nothing.

Wit. Right! and if you had common sense, I am sure you would never have made it; not but to do you justice, Sir Gilbert, I must own you have wit in your way too, though it's of a very odd turn, I grant you.

' *Sir Gilb.* Sir, I disown my pretensions to any, if ever
' you had sense enough to find it out.

' *Wit.* Sure you forget, my dear Sir Gilbert. Don't
' you remember once I did find it out? Did not I slily
' catch you in St. What-de-callum's churchyard, with
' your table book, taking dead people's names from the
' tomb-stones, to fill up your list of your third subscrip-
' tion, that you might be sure of those that would never
' come to claim it? and then pretended to all your
' friends you were full? There, at least, you had more
' wit to keep people out, than any man living had to
' get in : for I grant you, your list was dead sure! ha,
' ha, ha!

' *Sir Gilb.* Why, ay, this nonsensical story now passes
' for wit, I warrant, among your cockade and velvet
' sparks at Garraway's; but much good may do you
' with your jest, as long as we have your money among
' us : I believe it will be no hard matter to bite most of
' your soft heads off before it be long; and if you
' drive on as you seem to do, we shall make bold to set
' some of you down where we took you up, odsheart-
' likins.

' *Wit.* Nay, I grant you, to do your own business,
' you must do other peoples too ; but if all the young
' fellows of dress and pleasure would follow me, I would
' undertake to lead you a dance for all that.

' *Sir Gilb.* And, pray, what would you have them
' do!

' *Wit.* Why, do as you do: nothing that you pre-
' tend to do; or do as I did, every thing as you whif-
' pered me not to do. I minded what your broker did,
' not what you said, my dear! And if every gentle-
' man would but buy, when you advise him to sell; or
' sell when you advise him to buy, 'twould be impossible
' to go out of the way : why, 'tis as plain road, man,
' as from Hyde-Park corner to Kensington.'

Sir

Sir Gilb. Sir, you take a great deal of liberty with me; insomuch, that I must tell you, I am not sure I won't pay the forfeit of my contract, rather than part with my daughter to a coxcomb——and so take it as you will.

L. Wrang. Mr. Wrangle! what do you mean by this brutality?

Fran. Mr. Witling, Madam, will take nothing ill, that I think fit to justify, I am sure.

Wit. No, faith! you need not fear it; I'll marry before I'll fight, depend upon't. Ha, ha!

L. Wrang. Mr. Witling, I beg you come away this moment——I'll undertake to do your merit justice. I'll see who dares pretend to govern in this family beside myself. Charlotte, give him your hand—Come, Sir——

[*Exit Lady* Wrangle.

Wit. I am all obedience, Madam—your humble servant, Mr. Frankly——" Would you woo her——"

[*Exit, singing with* Charlotte.

Fran. Admirably well done, Sir! ' you have worked ' his insolence to rare order.' Now, if you can but stand it out as stoutly with my lady, our business is done.

Sir Gilb. If!—Will you stand by me?

Fran. Will you give me your authority, Sir, to handle her roundly, and make her know who ought to be her master?

Sir Gilb. My authority! ay, and thanks into the bargain——Come along,-I'll send for the lawyer now—— Mr. Frankly, my blood rises at her; she shall find I'll vindicate the honour of the city, and, from this moment, demolish her petticoat government.

Fran. Well said; I'll warrant you, Sir. [*Exeunt.*

END of the FOURTH ACT.

ACT V.

Sir Gilbert *and* Frankly.

SIR GILBERT.

MY dear Frankly, I could not rest till I had thee alone again; thou hast gained upon me for ever: your vindicating the husband's authority, and taking my

G

wife

wife a peg lower before my face, has tickled my fancy
to that degree, that, odzooks! I could wish in my heart
thou hadst been married to her.

Fran. Oh, I should be loth to have robbed you, Sir, of
that happiness.

Sir Gilb. A hum! you are right, you are right; I did
not think of that indeed. Well; it's a very odd thing
now, that a wife will sooner be kept under by any man
than her husband: why the deuce can't I govern her so?

Fran. There's no great secret in the matter, Sir; for
take any couple in Christendom, you will certainly find,
that the more troublesome of the two is always head of
the family.

Sir Gilb. By my troth, I believe you are right; and
since the war is begun, I'll make a fair push for't. I am
resolved now to thwart her in every thing; and if Granger has but wit enough to talk Sophronia into her senses;
that is, if he can but convince her that she is flesh and
blood, and born to breed, like other women; odzooks!
he shall marry her immediately: I'll plague her Ladyship
that way too.

‘ *Fran.* That way! Oh, ay, its true: for I think I
‘ have heard you say, Sir, that if either of your daugh-
‘ ters die unmarried, my Lady is to inherit their fortunes.

‘ *Sir Gilb.* Ay, ay; there the shoe pinches, man; she
‘ would be as much an enemy to Granger, as she is to
‘ you, if she could in the least suspect he would ever make
‘ any thing of it with Sophronia.’

Fran. And, if I don't mistake, Sir, Granger is in a fair
way there too; for, to my knowledge, he has been lock-
ed up with her this half hour, here in her library.

Sir Gilb. The dickens!

Fran. Did not you observe them steal off together, just
before the music?

Sir Gilb. I wondered, indeed, what was become of
them; by the lord Harry I am glad of it——I must have
a peep at them. [*Goes to the key-hole.*] Odso! they are
just a coming forth.

Fran. We had best be out of the way then, that we
may not disturb them.

Sir Gilb. No, no, I'll warrant you: pr'ythee, let us
stand ‘ behind this skreen,’ and observe what passes.

Fran.

Fran. Quick! quickly then; here they come.

[*They retire.*

Enter Granger *with* Sophronia.

Soph. Oh, Granger! still preserve this purity,
And my whole soul will open to receive thee:
Forget, like me, thy sex, how sweetly may
We pass our days in rational desire!
' Thou seest, I own, without a blush, my love,
' For blushes only rise from guilty flames;
' When conscience driven, reluctant to the crime,
' Leaps to the face, and marks the cheek with shame:
' But the chaste heart sublim'd by purer fires,
' Knowing no conscious fear, reserve, or guile,
' Gives, with unbounded frankness, all its store,
' And only blushes—that it gives no more.'

Gran. Hear this, ye bright immortal choirs above,
And own that human souls, like you, can love.

Sir Gilb. Heyday! this is downright love in a trage-
dy! Well; he's a comical thief.

' *Fran.* Hush! let him go on, Sir.

' *Soph.* Can you forgive the tedious banishment,
' Which my distrust and dread impos'd on you?

' *Gran.* Can I reproach you for so just, so kind
' A fear? While through the general race of man,
' A sensual and infectious passion rages,
' Giving, from sex to sex, the mortal tainture;
' Can I complain, if, to preserve yourself
' From the contagion, you've perhaps enjoin'd
' The healthy to perform his quarantine?
' But landing thus, upon my native soil,
' I leave my sufferings past behind, and think
' The present now is all that's left of time,
' Or worth my care.

' *Soph.* Blush! blush! ye base degenerate world,
' That boast the bliss of gross connubial love:
' Can you wear human forms, yet see the prone,
' The brute creation equal your desires?
' Had you or souls or sense refin'd, you'd form
' Your wishes worthy your superior being;
' Curb, with imperial reason, lawless nature,
' And reach, like us, the joys of love seraphic.'

Gran. Oh, harmony of heart! Oh, spotless passion!

G 2 Here,

Here, on this hand, the altar of my vows,
I offer up my purer part, my foul
To thine, and fwear inviolable———
   Soph. ——————————Hold !
Paffions, like ours, no formal vows require ;
For vows fuppofe diftruft, or faithlefs love,
The frail fecurity of fenfual flames ;
But where the pure, with the pure foul unites,
The fimple hand, thus given, and receiv'd, fuffices.
   Gran. Let then this hand my fpotlefs heart refign.
   Soph. Thus in exchange I blend my foul with thine.
   Sir Gilb. So ; they are got to hand and heart already ;
but now, now for a touch at the reft of her premifes.
   Fran. Nay, dear Sir, be eafy.
   Sir Gilb. Well ! well ! I will.
   Soph. And now, no more Sophronia, but thy friend ;
Be both my name and fex from hence forgotten.
   Gran. No :
Let me remember ftill that thou art fair ;
For were there no temptation in thy beauty,
Where were the merit of fuch hard refiftance ?
Indeed, my friend, 'tis hard ! 'tis hard refiftance !
' The organs of my fight, my ear, my feeling,
' As I am made of human mold, in fpite
' Of me, exert their functions, and are pleas'd :'
I view thee with delight, I hear with tranfport,
And thy touch——is rapture———
   ' *Soph.* How fares my friend ?
   ' *Gran.* Like the poor wretch that parches in a fever,
' With fatal thirft, yet begs for prefent eafe
' To drink, and die——
   ' *Soph.* From whence this new diforder ?
   ' *Gran.* Tell me, Sophronia, is my virtue blameful,
' Becaufe my fenfes act as nature bids them ?
' Am I in fault, if the fharp winter's froft
' Can chill my limbs, or fummer's fun will fcorn them ?
' What matter can refift the elements ?
' Rivers will freeze, and folid mountains burn ;
' What bodies will not change ?—Thus the tall oak—
   ' Though from our meaner flames fecure,
   ' Muft that, which falls from heaven, endure.
   ' *Soph.* Where has he learned this art of unoffending
' flattery ?   [*Afide.*
                      ' *Gran.*

' *Grang.* Canſt thou reproach me then, if while thy
    beauties
' With ſuch a blaze of charms invade my ſenſe,
' My human heart's not proof againſt their pow'r ?
  ' *Soph.* Reproach thee ! No ; bodies are but the ſhells,
' Or huts, that cover in the ſoul, and are,
' Like other fabrics, ſubjeċt to miſchance :
' The cells of hermits may be fir'd ; but none
' Reproach the wretch that ſuffers by the flame.'
    Gran. Oh, Sophronia ! canſt thou forgive me then,
That my material droſs thus burns before thee ?
That my whole frame thus kindles at thy beauty ?
And even warms my ſoul with fond deſire ?
' Like an impatient child it languiſhes,
' And pines for wants unknown, it ſighs, it pants,
' To be indulg'd upon thy friendly boſom,
' To fold thee in my tender arms, to talk,
' And gaze, with mutual ſoft benevolence
' Of eyes, as giving were our only pleaſure.'
    Sir Gilb. Adod ! I believe he's in earneſt, he makes
me half in love to hear him.
    Soph. Is it poſſible ? Can then.
Such ſoftneſs mingle with corporeal paſſion ?   [*Apart.*
    Gran. But while the ſoul alone is ſuffered to
Poſſeſs, and bars my mortal part from joy ;
My poor repining ſenſes murmur at
Their fate, and call thy purity unjuſt,
' To ſtarve the body, while the mind knows plenty,
' Yet, like a churl, ingroſſes whole the feaſt.
' My ſenſes claim a ſhare from nature's law ;
' They think, with a more melting ſoftneſs, they
' Could love, and e'en inform the ſoul with rapture.'
    Sir Gilb. Ay ; now we begin to work her.
' *Gran.* Conſider then, as part of me, thy friend,
' Thy friend may ſure be truſted with your pity !
' Oh, relieve them ! give me ſome ſign at leaſt,
' One kind embrace, or a chaſte ſiſter's kiſs,
' In certain proof that thou art ſtill my friend,
' That yet thou hat'ſt me not——I aſk no more.
    ' *Soph. Pignora certa petis? do pignora certa--Timendo.*
    Gran. ' Does then thy fear alone refuſe me ?' Oh,
    Sophronia !
                            G 3   Why,

Why, why muſt virtue be this foe to nature?
Why ſet our ſenſes with our ſouls at variance,
As Heav'n had form'd thee fair—to kill thy friend.

Soph. What means my throbbing heart? Oh, virtue!
Now ſave me from unequal nature's power! [now,
Now guard me from myſelf——and hide my ſhame!

Gran. Muſt I then periſh? Will my friend forſake me?

Soph. Oh, Granger! I am loſt!—thou haſt undone
I am fallen, and thou wilt hate me now. [me!

Gran. Oh, Sophronia!

Soph. ——Lend me thy arm, ſupport me!
Thy melting plaints have ſtole upon my heart,
And ſoften me to wiſhes never known before.

Gran. Oh, the tumultuous joy! [*She ſinks into his arms.*

Sir Gilb. Ah, dead! dead! We have her, boy! we
have her.

'*Gran.* See how ſhe pants!
' How, like a wounded dove, ſhe beats her wings,
' And trembling hovers to her mate for ſuccour.
' Oh, the dear confuſion! Awake, Sophronia!
' Now wake to new and unconceiv'd delights,
' Which faint philoſophy could never reach,
' Which nature gave thee charms to taſte and give.
'*Soph.* Oh, I cou'd wiſh, methinks, for ev'ry power,
' That might have charms for thee: thy words,
' Like Hybla drops, diſtil upon my ſenſe,
' And I could hear thee talk for ever.'

Gran. ' Oh, be but thus for ever kind, thy eyes
' Will find new ſubjects for eternal talk,
' And everlaſting love:' bluſh not, my fair,
That thou art kind; thy heart has only paid
To love, the tribute due from nature's whole creation:
' For wiſdom to his power oppos'd, is folly:'
Hear how the Britiſh Virgil ſings his ſway;
    " Thus every creature, and of every kind,
    The ſecret joys of mutual paſſion find;
    Not only man's imperial race, but they
    That wing the liquid air, or ſwim the ſea,
    Or haunt the deſert, ruſh into the flame;
    For love is lord of all, and is in all the ſame."

                    [*Exeunt* Gran. *and* Soph.
                                        Sir

Sir Gilb. Oh, rare philofophy! Oh, fine philofophy! dainty philofophy! ho! [*Singing.*

Fran. Ha, ha, ha! that muft be a pleafant fort of philofophy indeed, Sir, that pretends to be wifer than nature. Platonic love is a mere philofopher's ftone; when different fexes once come to lay their heads together about it, the projection's fure to fly *in fumo.*

Sir Gilb. Fumo! Ay, I warrant you. A handfome wench, that fhuts herfelf up two or three hours with a young fellow, only out of friendfhip, is making a hopeful experiment in natural philofophy indeed —— Why it's juft like fpreading a bag of gunpowder before a great fire, only to dry it; ha, ha, ha!

' *Fran.* Right, Sir—It puts me in mind of the Irifh
' foldier, who, to fteal powder out of a full barrel, cun-
' ningly bored a hole in it with a red hot poker.

' *Sir Gilb.* Ah, very good! ha, ha, ha! As you fay,
' it's hard luck indeed, that her firft touch of his hand
' fhould blow up all the reft of her body.

' *Fran.* But to do her juftice, Sir, fhe was not won
' without a good deal of art neither: a plain battery of
' love would have done nothing upon her; you fee, he
' was forced to fap her with his felf reproaches, and put
' it all upon the point of her compaffion to his fenfes.

' *Sir Gilb.* Nay, the toad did worm her nicely, that I
' muft needs fay.'

Fran. Ha, ha, ha! what a rare welcome too this news will have with my Lady! How fhe will fume at the difappointment!

Sir Gilb. Nay, I have nothing to do with that, you know; this was none of my doing: let every tub ftand upon its own bottom; ' I fhall e'en leave her Ladyfhip
' to his management: all I can promife him is, not to
' hinder the matter.

' *Fran.* That's all he will defire, I dare fay, Sir: be
' you but as a paffive in his affair as mine, I'll warrant
' we will find courage enough between us to maintain
' our pretenfions.

Enter a Servant.

Serv. Sir, here's Mr. Delay, the lawyer.

Sir Gilb. Odfo! that's well! Now, Mr. Frankly——
4
Fran.

Fran. I believe, Sir, you had beſt keep him out of my
Lady's fight, till matters are ripe for execution.

Sir Gilb. You are right, you are right ; ſay no more,
I'll do it. *Ah, the ſly rogue ! how he tickled her up !*

Fran. But harkee, harkee, Sir Gilbert—*don't flinch now ;
don't be a craven ; be ſure to ſtand it out ſtoutly with my
Lady.*

Sir Gilb. *Will you and Granger continue to ſtand by
me ?*

Fran. *To the laſt drop of our amorous blood to your
daughters, and our amiable blood to you.*

Sir Gilb. *Why then, if I don't ſquabble it out with her
Ladyſhip to the laſt drop of a huſband's authority, may I
live and die the cock of the hen-peck'd corporation.*

[*Exit.*

Fran. So ; thus far we ſtand fair : we have nothing
now to combat but my Lady ; and Granger's ſucceſs with
Sophronia, at this time, will naturally ſtrengthen our alliance againſt her. As for my friend Witling, his own
aſſurance and vanity will partly do his buſineſs : ' but,
' however, in the mean while, it will not be amiſs to
' keep him warm and ripe for our deſign'——*à-propos !*
here he comes.

Enter Witling.

Wit. Ha, ha, ha ! dear Tom ! I am glad I have found
thee, faith ! I have a favour to beg of thee.

Fran. Why then, I am glad you have found me too
——becauſe, I believe, I ſhall not grant it.

Wit. Ha, ha ! what crabbed ſtill, my dear ! But I
come to thee from a fair lady, child ; and 'tis for her ſake
I am going to be obliged to thee.

Fran. I am glad of that too. A woman of ſenſe, I
warrant her, by her ſending thee on a fool's errand.

' *Wit.* Ay, but my dear ! the errand happens to be
' her's now ; and ſo thou haſt civilly put the fool upon
' the woman of ſenſe. Good again ! one of thy old blun-
' ders, Tom ! for, I think thou haſt but curſed luck in
' making thy way to the women.

' *Fran.* When you tell me the lady you come from,
' I ſhall be better able to gueſs, whether ſhe takes me or
' you for a fool.'

Wit. Suppoſe then it were from a lady, Tom, that deſigns

figns to take either you or me for a hufband ? What doft thou think of my little Charlotte, my dear Tommy ?

Fran. Why, if fhe takes thee for a hufband, I fhall think her a fool ; and if I fhould take thee for a wit, fhe would think me a fool: but by her fending thee to afk a favour of me, it's a fign fhe thinks thee a fool.

Wit. Ha, ha ! a very pretty parcel of crofs purpofes ; a fool and wit, and wit and fool ; and fhe, and thee, and me ! What ! art thou playing at huftle-cap with thy words, child ? ' Thou doft not expect I fhould take all
' thy jingle jumble for wit, doft thou ?
' *Fran.* No, faith ! if it be wit, I expect thou fhouldft
' not take it.
' *Wit.* With all my heart—Come, come, it fhall be
' wit then ; 1 will miftake it for once.'—But to bufinefs—the fair lady, my dear Tom—

Fran. Ay, what of her ?
' *Wit.* Why, poor foul, fhe defir'd me to come to
' you, and——
' *Fran.* And leave her to better company, ha !
' *Wit.* Look you, Tom, I know lofers ought to have
' leave to fpeak, and therefore, at prefent, you fhall have
' all the wit to yourfelf, my dear : but don't be uneafy
' at my happinefs, dear Tom ; for to tell you the truth,
' the creature is fo curfed fond of me, that fhe begins
' to grow troublefome already. Ha, ha, ha !
' *Fran.* Why don't you make yourfelf eafy then, and
' give her up to me ?
' *Wit.* No no ; I muft not break the poor fool's heart
' neither :' for you muft know, fhe is in a terrible taking about me.

Fran. How fo, Sir ?
Wit. Why fhe faid, juft now, fhe was afraid to marry me fo foon as to-night upon thy account.

Fran. Good ! then there may be hopes fhe will not marry thee upon any account.

Wit. No, don't flatter thyfelf neither, my dear Tommy ; for her concern at the bottom was all upon my account.

Fran. How does that appear ?
Wit. Why you know, fays fhe, after all, poor Frankly has fome fort of pretenfions to me : I don't know how it

was

was, fays fhe; but fome way or other he got in with my
father: fo I durft not wholly difcourage his addreffes.
Now, Frankly's of a furly temper, ' fays fhe? and,
' if I fhould marry you, in the heat of his difappoint-
' ment, he may fay or do fome rafh thing upon't:' and
I know, fays fhe, Mr. Witling, you are violent in your
nature too; and if matters fhould rife to a quarrel, nobody knows where the mifchief may end; the world will
certainly lay it all at my door——I fhould be the mife-
rableft creature alive—— therefore I beg you, fays fhe,
go to him from me, and try to make an amicable end of
the bufinefs; and the moment poor Frankly's made
eafy, fays fhe, I'll marry you the next hour, without any
referve in the whole world.

Fran. Why then, without any referve in the whole
world, pray tell the lady, that fhe may depend upon it
I am certainly eafy——becaufe I am fure fhe impofes
upon you.

Wit. Impofe upon me, child! ha, ha! that's pleafant
enough, ha, ha!

Fran. That is, fhe let's you impofe upon yourfelf,
which is the fame thing.

Wit. That may be, Tom; but the devil take me if I
can find it out: ' but, however, I am mighty glad you
' do, becaufe then I am fure, as long as you are eafy,
' you can't take it ill, if I fhould burft my ribs with
' laughing at your fancy.

' *Fran.* Oh, not in the leaft! and to increafe your
' mirth, Sir, I will be farther bold to tell you, fhe has as
' hearty a contempt for you, if poffible, as I have.

' *Wit.* Good again! Ha, ha, ha!

' *Fran.* Thou art a thing fo below all human confide-
' ration, thou haft not wherewithal to give a Spaniard
' jealoufy.

' *Wit.* Ah, poor Tom, if thou didft but know all now!
' Ha, ha!

' *Fran.* But to think thyfelf agreeable to her, thou muft
' have the impudence of a French Harlequin.

' *Wit.* Ah, dear Tom, thou charmeft me! for fince I
' find thou art not, in the leaft, uneafy at her engage-
' ment with me, to tell thee the truth. I have nothing
' elfe at prefent that can poffibly retard my happinefs.

' *Fran.*

' *Fran.* Why then, Sir, be as happy as you deferve;
' and pray let the lady know, as to any favour she defigns
' you, I am in perfect peace of mind and tranquility.

' *Wit.* And you really give me leave to tell her fo ?

' *Fran.* Tell her, I am more eafy than she herfelf will
' be, when she has married you.

' *Wit.* Why then' perish me, if thou art not one of the
beft-bred rivals in the whole world ! ha, ha, ha ! and
here she comes, faith, to thank thee for her part of the
confolation. Ha, ha !

Fran. Ha, ha !

Enter Charlotte.

Char. So, gentlemen, I am glad to find you in fuch
good humour.

Wit. O ! Madam, the deareft friends in the world :
I have obey'd your commands, and here's honeft Tom is
fo far from being uneafy at our marriage, that 'egad I
can't get him to believe it will ever come to any thing.

Char. O ! as to that, Mr. Frankly may think as he
pleafes ; but if he is not uneafy upon your account, that's
all I pretend to defire of him.

Wit. No, no, honeft Tom will give us no trouble, depend upon it.

Fran. Not I, upon my honour, Madam, ' for though
' I might be provoked to cut another man's throat, that
' should pretend to you, yet the value I have for Mr.
' Witling, fecures him from my leaft refentment.

' *Wit.* Look you there, Madam ! you fee your fears
' are all over ; I don't find we have any thing to do now,
' but to fend for the parfon.

' *Char.* Ay, but I don't well underftand him ; for he
' feems to be neither jealous of your merit, nor my in-
' clination : and that I can fcarce think poffible.

' *Fran.* You may, upon my foul, Madam : for I have
' fo juft a fenfe of both, that if it had not been in re-
' gard to your father's contract, I am convinced you
' would never have endured the fight of him.

' *Wit.* Ah ! poor Tom ! he has much ado to fmother
' it.   [*Apart.*

' *Char.* Very pretty ! fo you think that my admitting
' his addreffes is mere grimace, and that I am all this
' while taking pains only to deceive Mr. Witling.

' *Fran.* Alas ! you need not do that, Madam ; he takes fo
' much

' much to deceive himſelf, he really gives you no trouble
' about it.

' *Wit.* You ſee, child, we may put any thing upon
' him.

' *Char.* Right! you take it as I could wiſh! Let me
' alone with him. And ſo, Sir, you really expect I ſhould
' be pleaſed with your having this free opinion of my
' conduct?'

Fran. I muſt be pleaſed with every thing you undertake in my favour, Madam.

Wit. How vain the rogue is too! [*Aſide.*

Char. I am amaz'd! but how naturally a coxcomb
ſhews himſelf. [*Aſide.*

Wit. Ay, that's when he is in your hands, Madam;
' Ha, ha! 'Egad ſhe plays him nicely off. [*Aſide.*

' *Char.* After this, one ſhould wonder at nothing!
' Nay, there are ſome fools, I ſee, whoſe vanity is ſo far
' from being offenſive, that they become diverting even
' to a rival.

' *Fran.* Mr. Witling is always entertaining, Madam.

' *Wit.* Hah, prodigious! 'Egad he thinks you mean me
' all this while. Ha, ha, ha! [*Apart.*

' *Char.* Well, ſure there never was ſo bright a cox-
' comb! [*Apart.*

' *Wit.*' 'Egad I'll humour him: Ha, ha? [*Apart.*

Char. By all means, you will make him ſhine to a miracle. [*Apart.*

Wit. Why then, periſh me Tom, if ever I was ſo well
diverted at a French comedy. [*Shakes his hand.*

Fran. That may very well be, Sir; for fools are apt
to be fond of their own parts. [*Shakes Witling's hand.*

Char. Ha, ha!

Wit. Ay! ſo they are, the devil take me; for, I ſee,
there's no beating thee out of thine.

Fran. How ſhould I be out, when you play all the
ſcene yourſelf!

Wit. No, no, Tom, I only laugh all; but 'tis your
part that makes me, child.

Fran. Right! If you did not laugh, where the devil
ſhould the jeſt be?

Wit. Why, then, you ſee, I do the fool juſtice, Tom,
Ha, ha!

Fran.

Fran. Ay, the devil take me, doſt thou; I never ſaw him better acted.

' *Wit.* Ah! but you don't know, my dear, that to ' make a coxcomb ſhine, requires a little more wit than ' thou art aware of.

' *Fran.* I know that he who has leaſt wit of us two, ' has enough to do that, my dear.

' *Wit.* Ay, that is when a coxcomb ſhows himſelf, ' Tom.

' *Fran.* Nay, in that I grant no mortal can come up ' to thee.

' *Wit.* Ha, ha, ha! Oh, dear rogue, I muſt kiſs ' thee.

' *Omnes.* Ha, ha, ha!

Enter Lady Wrangle.

L. Wrang. Your ſervant, your ſervant, good people: whence all this mighty mirth, pray?

Wit. O, Madam, here has been ſuch a ſcene! ſuch hit and daſh upon one another; in ſhort, ſuch brightneſs o'both ſides, the full moon, in a froſty night, never came up to it,

Char. I muſt needs ſay, I never ſaw Mr. Witling ſhine ſo before.

' *Fran.* No, Madam? Why, he always talks like a lu- ' natic, as you now may judge by his ſimilies.

' *Wit.* Ah, poor Tom! thy wit indeed is, like the ' light of the moon, none of thy own: if I don't miſ- ' take, my dear, I was forced to ſhine upon thee, before ' thou wert able to make one reflection.

' *Fran.* There you are once in the right: for I certain- ' ly could not have laughed, if you had not given me a ' hearty occaſion.

' *Wit.* Ay, but the cream of the jeſt is, Tom, that at ' the ſame time I really gave thee no occaſion at all.

' *Fran.* Right again, my dear: for your not knowing ' that, is the only jeſt that's worth laughing at.

' *Both.* Ha, ha, ha!'

L. Wrang. This muſt be ſome extraordinary miſtake indeed; for I have no notion that Mr. Frankly and you can have reaſon to laugh upon the ſame occaſion.

Wit. Why, faith! the occaſion is a little extraordi-

H   nary;

nary; for you muſt know, Madam, that honeſt Tom and
I here, are both going to be married to this lady.

L. Wrang. Both!

Wit. Ay both, Madam; for, it ſeems, ſhe has not
been able to convince us, that either of us muſt go without her.

L. Wrang. That's ſo like Mr. Frankly's vanity, that
cannot think his miſtreſs loſt, though he ſees her juſt falling into the arms of his rival.

Fran. My vanity and yours, Madam, are much upon
a foot; tho' I think you happened to be firſt cured of it.

L. Wrang. What do you mean, Sir?

Fran. That by this time you are convinced I was never
in love with your ladyſhip.

L. Wrang. I am convinced, that a very little trouble
would have made you ſo.

' *Fran.* It muſt have been a good deal more than it coſt
' me, to make you believe ſo.

' *L. Wrang.* If you have ſtill hopes of marrying
' Charlote, Sir, I don't wonder at your believing any
' thing. Ha, ha, ha!

' *Fran.* Laugh when you ſee me deſpair, Madam.

' *L. Wrang.* I need not ſtay for that; your hope, is
' ridiculous enough, and I laugh becauſe you can't ſee.'

Fran. ' Yes, yes, I can ſee,' Madam: I have ſeen all
this day what 'tis you drive at: in ſhort, Madam, you
have no mind that either of Sir Gilbert's daughters ſhould
marry; becauſe if they die maids, you have ſecured the
chance of ſucceeding to their fortunes.

' *L. Wrang.* Ay, do make the world believe that, if
' you can: perſuade Mr. Witling that I have no mind
' Charlotte ſhould marry him.

' *Fran.* What Mr. Witling thinks, is out of the queſ-
' tion, Madam; but you are ſure that ſhe never deſigns to
' marry him: ſo that your ſetting up his pretenſions is
' not with the leaſt view of doing him good, but of doing
' me harm; or rather, that while you manage the diſ-
' pute well on both ſides, neither of us may have her.

' *L. Wrang.* He has gueſs'd the ſecret; but that ſhall
' not hinder my proceeding. [*Aſide.*] You are in the right
' to hope as long as you can, Sir; but I preſume you
                                              ' don't

' don't do it from my friendſhip, nor Mr. Wrangle's con-
' ſent, or Charlotte's inclination.

' *Fran.* Be what it will, Madam, it has a better foun-
' dation, than your hope of ſuceeding either to her's or
' Sophronia's fortune: for,' ſhall I tell you another ſecret, Madam? Sophronia is going to be married to
Granger; ſo that you are equally like to be diſappointed
there too.

L. Wrang. Sophronia married!

Fran. Ay, ay, married, married, Madam: wedded,
bedded, made a mere wife of: 'tis not half an hour ago
ſince I ſaw her ſink, and melt into his boſom, with all
the yielding fondneſs of a milk-maid.

L. Wrang. Sophronia, do this?

Fran. Sophronia, Madam; nay, Sir Gilbert was, at
the ſame time, a ſecret witneſs of all; and was glad, glad
of it, Madam: ' and to my certain knowledge, reſolves,
' that Granger ſhall marry her inſtantly:' and ſo, Madam,
all that fantaſtic ſort philoſophy, that you have been
building in her brains for ſeven years together, is (with
one honeſt attack of mere fleſh and blood) fairly demoliſh-
ed, and brought to nothing.

L. Wrang. I'll not believe it; I know your ears deceiv'd
you; he might perhaps tranſport her, but never to a ſenſual thought.

' *Fran.* Oons! Madam, I tell you, I heard and ſaw it
' all; myſelf, ſaw her ſighing, bluſhing, panting in his
' arms, with mortal, ſenſual, amorous deſire: all her
' romantic pride reduced, and humbled to the obedience
' of that univerſal monarch of mankind, Love, Madam;
' plain, naked, natural Love, Love, Madam.

' *L. Wrang.* I am confounded! If this be true, his
' triumph is inſupportable. [*Aſide.*] Ha! what do I ſee!'

Enter Granger, *leading* Sophronia.

' *Fran.* Dear Granger, I congratulate thy happineſs!

' *Gran.* My happineſs indeed! for till I was victorious,
' I know not half the value of my conqueſt.

' *Fran.* [*To* Sophronia.] Give me then leave to hope,
' Madam, that our former difference is forgot; ſince the
' more elevated paſſion of my friend has now convinced
' me of my own unworthineſs.

' *Soph.*

' *Soph.* I cannot difavow my tendereft fenfe of Gran-
' ger's merit, give it what name you pleafe; I own 'tis
' fomething——*Quod nequeo dicere, & fentio tantum :*
' but am proud that love alone, unaffifted by philofophy,
' could never have fubdued me.
' *L. Wrang.*' Is it poffible !
By your leave, Madam.
  [*She breaks through the company, and takes* Soph. *apart.*
' *Fran.* Heyday ! what's to do now ?
' *Gran.* O Frankly ! I have fuch a melting ⎫
' fcene to tell thee !   ⎪
' *Fran.* You may fpare yourfelf the trouble, ⎬ [*Afide.*
' Sir Gilbert and I over-heard every word of it. ⎪
' But I allow you an artift.   ⎪
' *Gran.* Was it not very whimfical ?   ⎪
' *Fran.* Hufh !   ⎭
' *L. Wrang.* [*To* Soph.'] Look in my face—full upon
me.
  Soph. Why that fevere look, Madam ?
  L. Wrang. To make you blufh at your apoftafy.
  Soph. Converts to truth are no apoftates, Madam.
  L. Wrang. Is this your felf-denial ! This your diftafte
of odious man ?
  Soph. Madam, I have confider'd well my female ftate,
and am now a profelyte to that philofophy, which fays,
        Nature makes nought in vain.
  L. Wrang. What's then become of your Platonic
fyftem ?
  Soph. Diffolved, evaporated, impracticable, and falla-
cious all : you'll own I have labour'd in the experiment,
but found at laft, that to try gold in a crucible of virgin-
wax, was a mere female folly.
  L. Wrang. But how durft you, Madam, entertain a
thought of marriage without acquainting me ?
  Soph. Madam, I am now under this gentleman's protection ; and from henceforth, think my actions only cog-
nizable to him.
  L. Wrang. Very fine !
  Fran. Ay, ay, Madam, 'tis but fretting your fpleen
to no purpofe ; you have no right to difpofe of either of
thofe ladies : Sir Gilbert's confent is what we depend
upon : and as far as that can go, we fhall make bold to
                                              infift

infift upon them both, Madam : and fo you may as well put your paffion in your pocket, Madam.

L. Wrang. Infupportable! [*Walks in anger.*

Wit. Ha, ha! well faid, Tommy! What, art thou crack-brained ftill, my dear? How the devil didft thou come by Sir Gill's confent? What, he has not mortgag'd it twice over, has he? But if he has, with all my heart; I fancy we fhall find a way to make his firft deed ftand good, however; and that, I am fure, I have here fafe in my pocket, child.

Fran. Oh, that fhall be tried prefently, Sir; and here he comes with the lawyer, for the purpofe.

Enter Sir Gilbert, *with a Lawyer.*

L. Wrang. Mr. Wrangle, what do you mean by this ufage? How dare you affront me thus?

Sir Gilb. I affront you, my Lady!

L. Wrang. Ay, Sir, by bringing thefe royfters here, to infult me in my own family.

Sir Gilb. Frankly—ftand by me.

Gran. Royfters, Madam!

L. Wrang. Sir, I am not fpeaking to you. I fay, Mr. Wrangle, how dare you do this?

Sir Gilb. Do, Madam! I don't do any thing, not I. If the gentlemen have done any harm, you had beft talk to them; I believe they have both tongues in their heads, and will be able to anfwer you.

Fran. Ay, ay, Madam, if you have received any in- jury from either of us, we are the proper perfons to talk with you.

L. Wrang. What, will you ftand by, and tamely fee me abufed in my own houfe?

Sir Gilb. Odzines, Madam, don't abufe yourfelf! the gentlemen are civil gentlemen, and men of honour; but if you don't know how to behave yourfelf to them, that's none of their fault.

L. Wrang. Prodigious! behave myfelf! Do you pre- fume to teach me, you rude, illiterate monfter?

Sir Gilb. Hold her faft, pray, gentlemen.

Gran. [*Interpofing.*] Come, come, be compofed, Ma- dam. Confider how thefe violent emotions difhonour your philofophy.

Sir Gilb. Ay, Madam, if you are a philosopher, now, let's fee a fample of it.

L. Wrang. Yes, Sir, I'll give you one inftance of it immediately; before you ftir out of this room, I'll make you do juftice to this gentleman; I'll make you keep your contract, Sir.

Sir Gilb. Why, Madam, you need not be in a paffion about that; I don't defign any other; I'll do him juftice immediately.

L. Wrang. Oh, will you fo? Come, then, where's the deed, Sir?

Wit. A-hum! Your humble fervant! How doft thou do now, my little Tommy?

Fran. I'll tell you prefently, Sir.

Wit. Ha, ha! 'Egad, thou art refolved to die hard, I find.

Law. Here, Madam, this is the deed; there is nothing wanting but the blanks to be filled up with the bridegroom's name. Pray, which is the gentleman?

L. Wrang. Here, Sir, this is he——Put in William Witling, efq.

Sir Gilb. Hold, Madam, two words to that bargain? that is not the gentleman I have refolved upon.

L. Wrang. Come, come, Mr. Wrangle, don't be a fool, I fay.

Sir Gilb. And, pray, Madam, don't you pretend to be wifer than I am.

L. Wrang. What ftupid fetch have you got in your head now?

Wit. Heyday! what time of the moon is this? Why, have not I your contract here in my hand, Sir Gilbert?

Sir Gilb. With all my heart; make your beft on't; I'll pay the penalty; and what have you to fay now? And fo, Sir, [*To the Lawyer.*] I fay, put me in Thomas Frankly, efq.

L. Wrang. Mr. Wrangle, don't provoke me. Do you know that the penalty of your refufing Mr. Witling, is above fix-and-twenty thoufand pounds difference, Sir?

Sir Gilb. Yes, Madam; but to let you fee that I am not the fool you take me for, neither; there's that will fecure me againft paying a farthing of it.

[*Sir* Gilbert *fhews a bond.*

L. Wrang.

2

L. Wrang. What do you mean?

Sir Gilb. Why, that this, Madam, is a joint bond from Mr. Granger and Frankly, to indemnify me from all de-mands, costs, and consequences of Mr. Witling's contract.

[*Lady* Wrangle *peruses the bond.*

Char. Now, Mr. Witling, you see upon what a shal-low foundation Frankly built all his vanity and assurance. But, poor man! he did not consider it was still in my power to marry you, tho' you had no contract at all with my father.

Wit. Right, my pretty soul—I suppose he thought the merit and frank air of this bond, forsooth, would have made you cock sure to him; but I'll let him see, pre-sently, that I know how to pay a handsome compliment to a fair lady, as well as himself. 'Egad, I will bite his head off.

Char. Ay, do, Mr. Witling; you touch my heart with the very thought of it.

Wit. Ah, you charming devil!

L. Wrang. [*To Sir* Gilbert.] Is this, then, your expe-dient? Is this your sordid way of evading all right and justice? Go, you vile scandal to the board you sit at! But you shall find that I have a superior sense of honour: and thus, thus, thus, I'll force you to be just.

[*Tears the bond.*

Fran. Confusion!

Sir Gilb. Oons, Madam! what do you mean by this outrage?

L. Wrang. Now, where's your security? Where is your vile evasion now, Sir? What trick, what shift have you now to save you?

Sir Gilb. Frankly——stand by me.

' *Fran.* Was ever such a devil?'

Gran. Fear nothing; I'll warrant you; come, Sir, don't be disheartened; your security shall be renewed to your content. Let the lawyer draw it up this instant, and I'll give my word and honour to sign it again before all this company.

Sir Gilb. Say'st thou so, my lad? Why, then, odsheart-likins——Frankly, stand by me.

Fran. Generous Granger!

L. Wrang. Let the lawyer draw up any such thing in my house, if he dares.　*Gran.*

Gran. Nay, then, Madam, I'll fee who dares moleſt him.

Fran. 'Egad, whoever does, ſhall have more than one to deal with.

Sir Gilb. Well ſaid ; ſtand your ground—Write away, man.   [*To the Lawyer.*

Char. Now, Mr. Witling————

Wit. Nay, nay, if that's your play, gentlemen—Come, come, I'll ſhew you a ſhorter way to make an end of this matter———and to let you fee you are all in the wrong box, and that now I am fecure of the lady's inclination, I think it a diſhonour to her beauty to make uſe of any other advantage, than the naked merit of her humble ſervant. There, Sir Gilbert, there's your contract back again ; tear it, cancel it, or light your pipe with it—And Madam————   [*To* Char.

Char. Ay, now, Mr. Witling, you have made me the happieſt creature living. And now, Mr. Lawyer———

Wit. Ay, now, gentlemen———

Char. Put in Thomas Frankly, eſq.

Wit. Fire and brimſtone !

Fran. Ay, now Mr. Witling————

Sir Gilb. Odſheart, in with him————

L. Wrang. Come, come, Mr. Wrangle————

Sir Gilb. Oons, wife, be quiet !

L. Wrang. Wife ! What, am I abuſed, inſulted, then ?

Sir Gilb. Ah, Charlotte, let me hug thee, and buſs thee, and bleſs thee to death ! But, here, huſſy, here's a pair of lips that will make better work with thee.

Wit. Bit, by the powers !

Char. Nay, don't ſay that of me, Mr. Witling ; 'twas even all your own doing : for you can't reproach me with having once told you I ever loved, or liked you. How then could you think of marrying me ?

Wit. Not reproach you, Madam ? Oons, and death ! did you not as good as————

Fran. Hold, Sir ; when you ſpeak to my wife, I muſt beg you to ſoften the tone of your voice a little.

Wit. Heyday ! what a pox, muſt not loſers have leave to ſpeak, neither ?

Fran. No, no, my dear Billy, thou art no loſer at all ;

for

for you have made your call, you fee, and now have fairly had your refufal too.

Wit. Ha, ha! that's pleafantly faid, however, 'egad! I can't help laughing at a good thing, though, tho' I am half ready to hang myfelf.

Fran. Nay, then, Witling, henceforth I'll allow thee a man of parts; ' tho', at the fame time, you muft grant ' me, there are no fools like your wits.' But fince thou haft wit enough to laugh at thyfelf, I think nobody elfe ought to do it.

' *Wit.* Why, then, dear Tom, I give you joy; for, to ' fay the truth, I believe I was a little over-hafty in this ' matter. But, as thou fayeft, he that has not wit ' enough to find himfelf fometimes a fool, is in danger of ' being fool enough to have nobody think him a wit but ' himfelf.'

Fran. [*To L.* Wrang.] And now, Madam, were it but poffible to deferve your pardon——

L. Wrang. I fee you know my weaknefs——Submiffion muft prevail upon a generous nature—I forgive you.

Sir Gilb. Why, that's well faid of all fides. And, now you are part of my family, gentlemen, I'll tell you a fecret that concerns your fortunes——Hark you—in one word——fell——fell out as faft as you can; for (among friends) the game's up——afk no queftions——but, I tell you, the jeft is over——But money down, (d'ye obferve me?) money down. Don't meddle for time; for the time's a coming, when thofe that buy will not be able to pay. And fo, the devil take the hindmoft; and Heaven blefs you all together.

Gran. And now, Sophronia, fet we forward to the promifed land of love.

Soph. In vain, againft the force of nature's law,
    Would rigid morals keep our hearts in awe;
    All our loft labours of the brain but prove,
    In life there's no philofophy like love.

END of the FIFTH ACT.

EPILOGUE.

THE time is come the Roman bard foretold,
  A brazen year succeeds an age of gold;
An age ——
When specious books were open'd for undoing,
And English hands, in crouds, subscrib'd their ruin.
Some months ago, whoever could suppose,
A goosequill race of rulers should have rose,
T'have made the warlike Britons groan beneath their blows?
Evils, that never yet beheld the sun,
To foreign-arms, or civil jars, unknown,
These trembling miscreants, by their wiles have done.
Thus the fierce lion, whom no force could foil,
By village-curs is baited in the toil.
Forgive the muse then, if her scenes were laid
Before your fair possessions were betray'd;
She took the flitting form as fame then ran,
While a director seem'd an honest man:
But were she from his present form to take him,
What a huge gorging monster must she make him?
How would his paunch with golden ruin swell?
Whole families devouring at a meal?
What motley humour in a scene might flow,
Were we these upstarts in their arts to show?
When their high betters at their gates have waited,
And all to beg the favour to be cheated;
Even that favour, (or they're by fame bely'd)
To raise the value of the cheat, deny'd.
And while Sir John was airing on his prancers,
He'as left his cookmaid to give peers their answers.
Then clerks in Berlins, purchas'd by their cheats,
That splash their walking betters in the streets.
And while, by fraud, their native country's sold,
Cry, Drive, you dog, and give your horses gold:
Even Jews no bounds of luxury refrain,
But boil their Christian hams in pure Champain.
Till then, the guilty, that have caus'd these times,
Feel a superior censure for their crimes,
Let all, whose wrongs the face of mirth can bear,
Enjoy the muse's vengeance on them here.

www.ingramcontent.com/pod-product-compliance
Lightning Source LLC
Chambersburg PA
CBHW031441270326
41930CB00007B/821